Praise for
The Genesis of Violence

"A deeply touching work of art with crafted words and images that reach into the places that matter and from the heart calling to the mind to both confess and repent. I loved this simply profound work and hope it to be the first of more!"

Wm. Paul Young
Author of *The Shack*

"A wonderfully imaginative retelling of the central themes of Genesis for all ages. The mixture of a judiciously pared-down text and extraordinarily evocative and appropriate artwork brings out with great clarity the ways in which imitation and violence structure some of our greatest ancient stories. They reveal how much those stories, told in this way, have to offer us."

James Alison
Catholic Priest, Theologian, and Author

"In an era when organized religion, especially Western religion, is being rejected by many, Distefano and Parsons present a needed reminder of the original merit and beauty of the biblical creation myths. The centering of human and Divine love and reconciliation instead of wrath and estrangement is welcome and needed. This reminds Christians that human love and forgiveness can come about outside of the popular substitutionary atonement story. A needed dose of humility and reminder of God's consistent love and the capacity for humans to embrace it and each other."

Rev. Roger Wolsey
Author of *Kissing Fish: Christianity for People Who Don't Like Christianity*

"*The Genesis of Violence* is perhaps the most unexpected book anyone would ever anticipate from the mind of Matthew Distefano. It's not irreverent. It's not snarky. There are no F-bombs to drop. In truth, *The Genesis of Violence* is actually a very beautiful, profound and, dare I say, 'Christian' book, gorgeously illustrated by Zak D. Parsons, that reframes the Genesis narrative into a visual storybook for adults that even your mom would love."

KEITH GILES

Author of the 7-part *Jesus Un* book series

"Matthew Distefano and Zak Parson's *The Genesis of Violence* is a refreshing and illuminating work. Though brief, it leaves you with a belly full of thought and evocation of emotion. Through the simple yet complex illustrations, it captures the brevity of life, its fleeting joys and unavoidable pains. Through its pronouncement of a story that we tend to see as rote, we are refreshed with the facts that we in humanity all face an inevitable invitation: that we should all practice more kindly and considerate thought toward each other. This beautiful work will awaken and remind us all to use our best gifts and offerings to help our fellow travelers on the journey and to make the path brighter and easier. It will foster a closer kinship, more empathy and a deeper understanding for each of us who want to live an extraordinary life and die knowing we did our very best to leave humanity greater."

NORA SOPHIA

Survivor, Author, and Teacher whose passion is to heal humanity with harmony

"Through a combination of evocative images and text, this book challenges readers to reimagine the violence in Genesis as a product of humankind's misguided search for God rather than God's unrelenting judgments against humanity."

KEVIN MILLER

Author and Filmmaker

The Genesis of Violence

Matthew J. Distefano
AND
Zak D. Parsons

All rights reserved. No part of this book may be used or reproduced, stored in a retrieval system, or transmitted in any form or by any means, electronic, mechanical, photocopying, recording, scanning, or otherwise, without written permission from the publisher except in the case of brief quotations embodied in critical articles and reviews. Permission for wider usage of this material can be obtained through Quoir by emailing permission@quoir.com.

Copyright © 2021 by Matthew J. Distefano and Zak D. Parsons.

First Edition

Cover design and layout by Rafael Polendo (polendo.net)
Illustrations by Zak D. Parsons (zakdp.com)

ISBN 978-1-957007-02-1

This volume is printed on acid free paper and meets ANSI Z39.48 standards.
Printed in the United States of America

Published by Quoir
Oak Glen, California
www.quoir.com

Dedicated to
Lyndsay and Heather

Table of Contents

Foreword by Adam Ericksen 9

Chapter I: In the Beginning 11

Chapter II: Blood and Sacrifice 27

Chapter III: The Call of the Patriarch 43

Chapter IV: Sibling Rivalry 57

Chapter V: Treachery and Reconciliation 71

Foreword

The book of Genesis is full of jealousy, rivalry, and violence. No wonder it has captured the imagination of readers for thousands of years.

It only takes four chapters for the first brothers to succumb to jealousy and murder in the name of God. And only two chapters later for violence to spread to apocalyptic proportions.

Many people today think that the Bible is irrelevant. But all anyone needs to do is read the first book of the Bible and watch the evening news to discover that Genesis' description of the human condition is as relevant as ever.

But Genesis doesn't just describe the human condition; it also delivers the prescription for the jealousy, rivalry, and violence that plagues us.

As Matthew and Zak show in this beautiful book, the prescription begins with the gradual recognition that the problem is human. God is not violent, nor does God desire violence. Genesis reveals the human propensity to project our own violence onto God, but it also reveals God's desire for us to stop our violence so that we can live with one another in relationships of love, forgiveness, and reconciliation.

Matthew has beautifully clarified the wisdom of anti-sacrifice and anti-violence that runs throughout Genesis. Once Matthew has opened our eyes to the nonviolent wisdom at the heart of this book, you cannot unsee it. Zak's beautiful artwork is an illuminating companion as we discover the heart of the true God who never wanted violence or sacrifice, but always wanted love

May you discover that love in an ever-deepening way as you read this book.

ADAM ERICKSEN

Pastor and Executive Director at The Raven Foundation

Chapter I

In the Beginning

In the beginning,

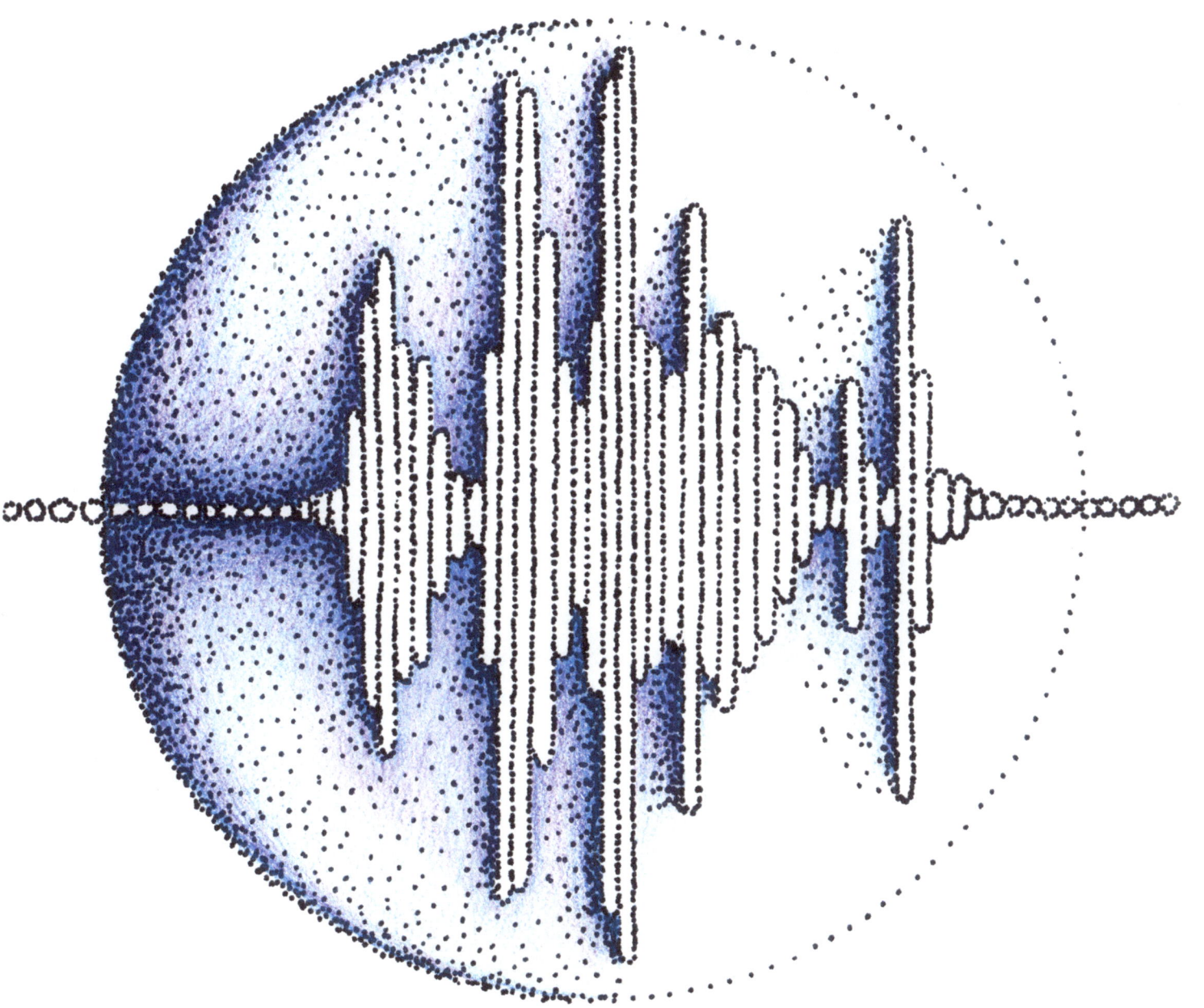

God spoke.

THE GENESIS OF VIOLENCE

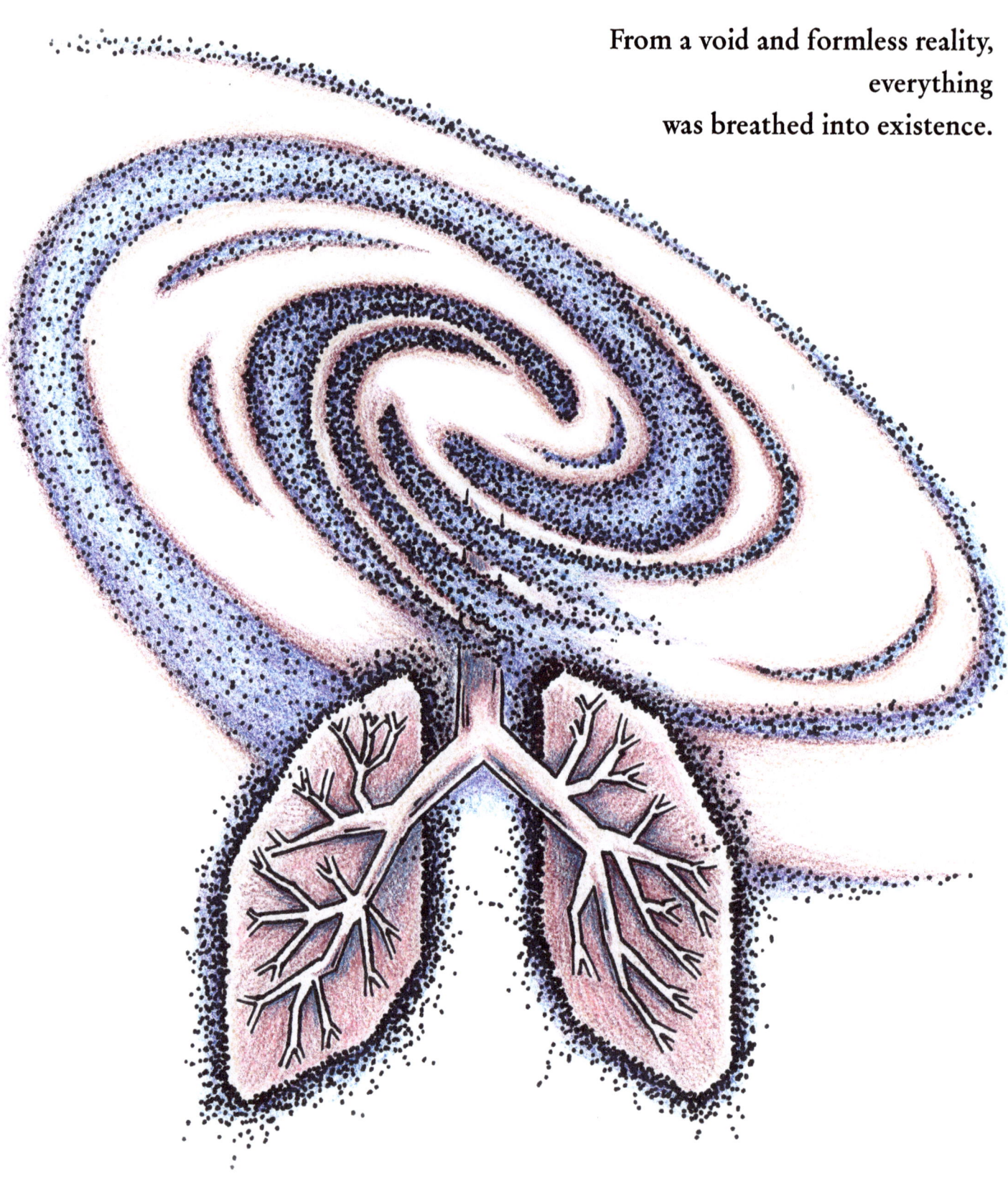

From a void and formless reality, everything was breathed into existence.

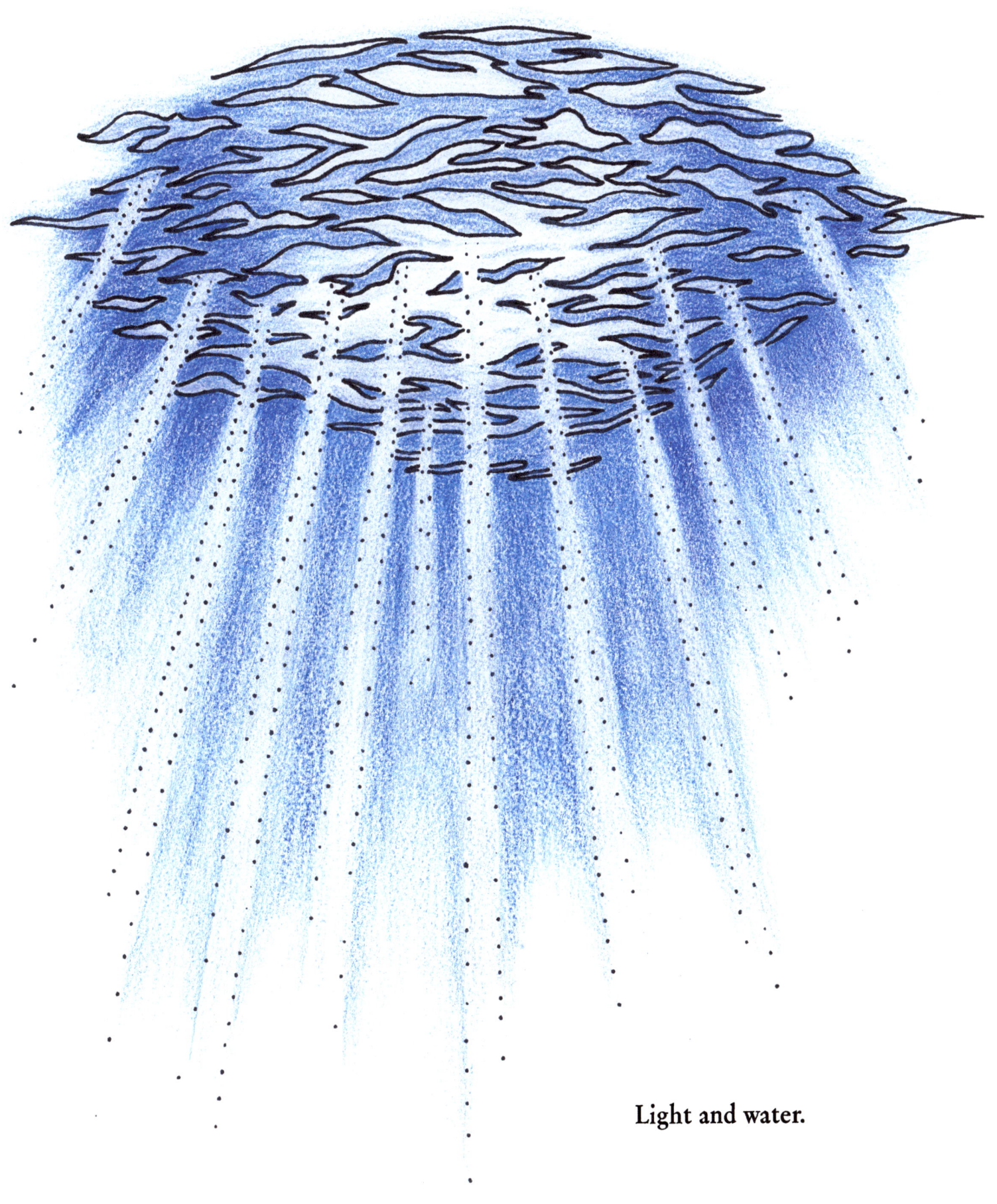

Light and water.

Earth and vegetation.

The sun,
and moon,
and stars.

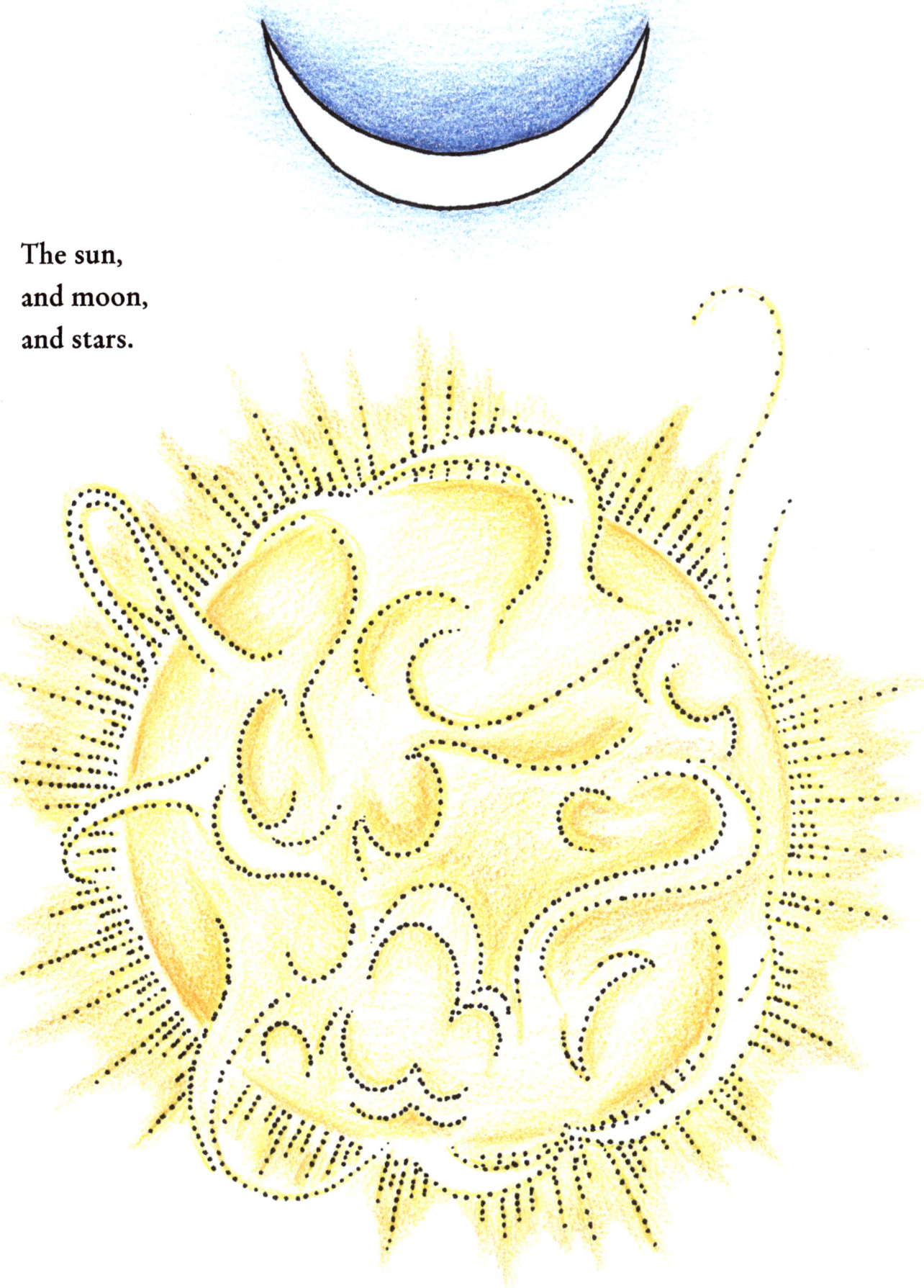

Creatures of the earth;

Creatures of the sea.

And then ...

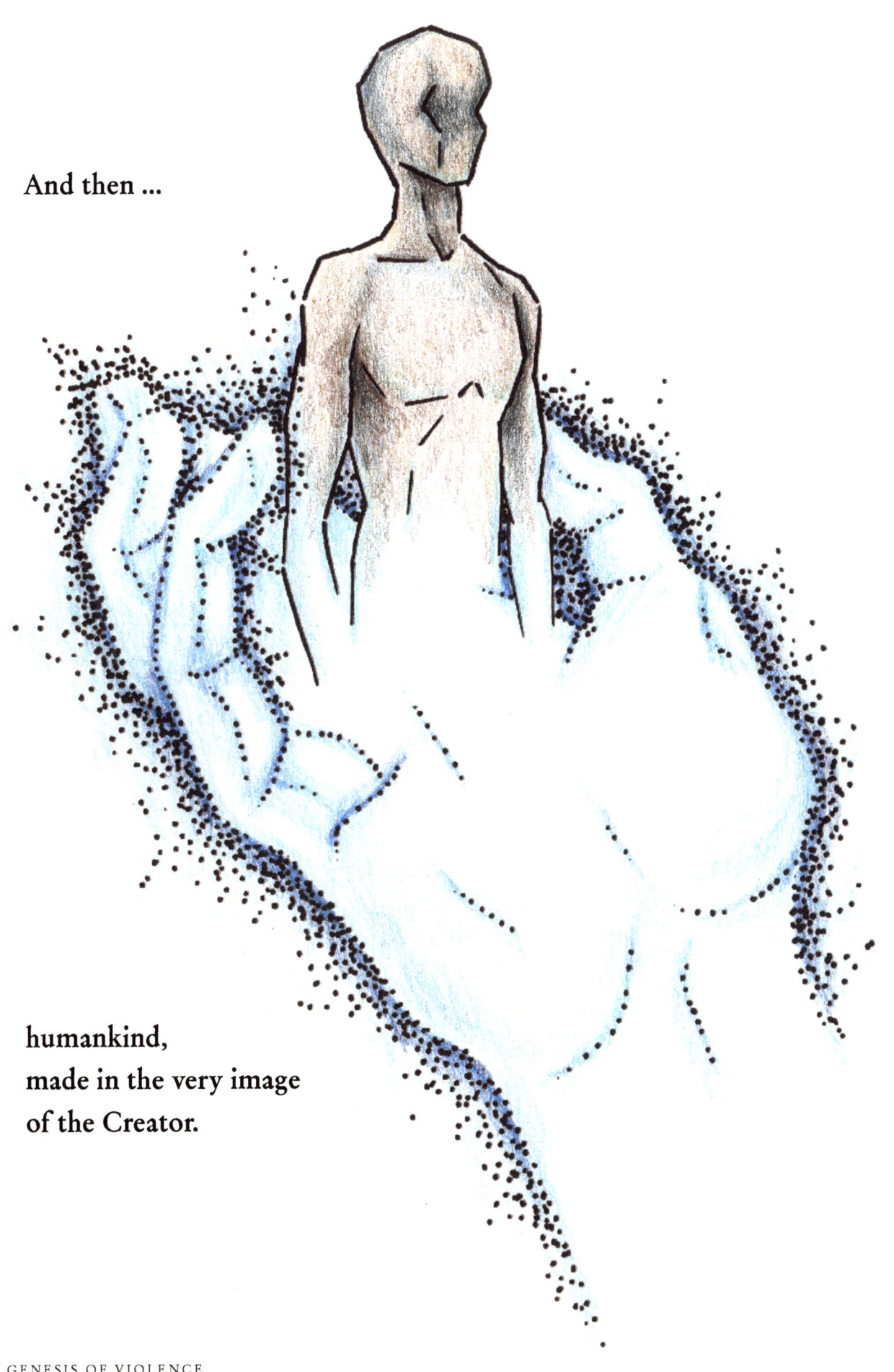

humankind,
made in the very image
of the Creator.

THE GENESIS OF VIOLENCE

The task for humanity?
> Fill the earth and care for it,
>> delighting in her bounty.

But this would prove to be a most difficult task.

For humanity's desire was to become gods themselves, to possess the knowledge of good and evil. But it wasn't theirs to have.

And so, jealousy awakened in them, and over time, driven by their desire, they set down their gnarled roots of malice against the Creator.

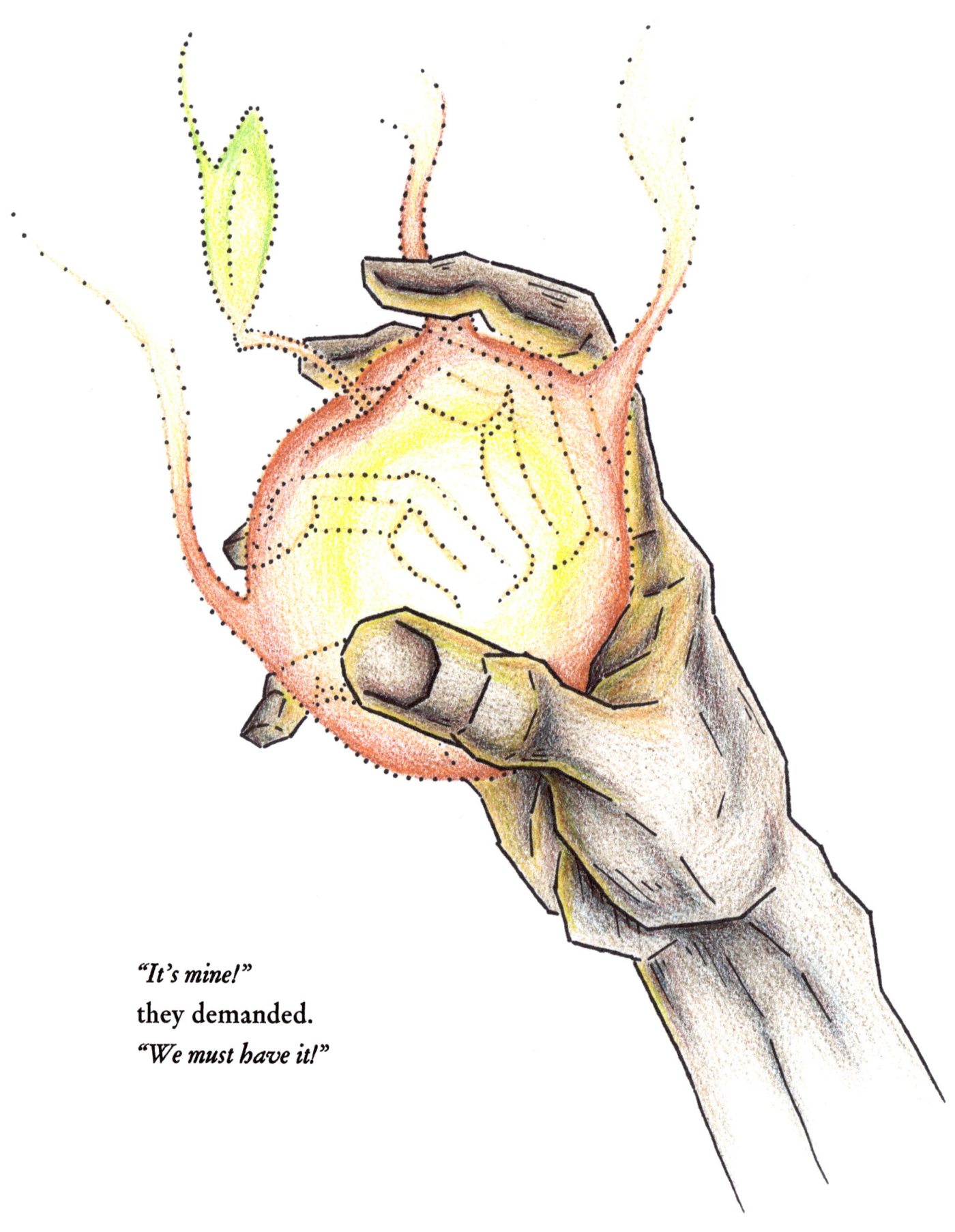

"It's mine!"
they demanded.
"We must have it!"

In their haste,
they grasped,
and ate from its fruit,
like vultures on carrion,

unceasingly.

After they ate,
the paradise humanity was given
would quickly become
something else ...

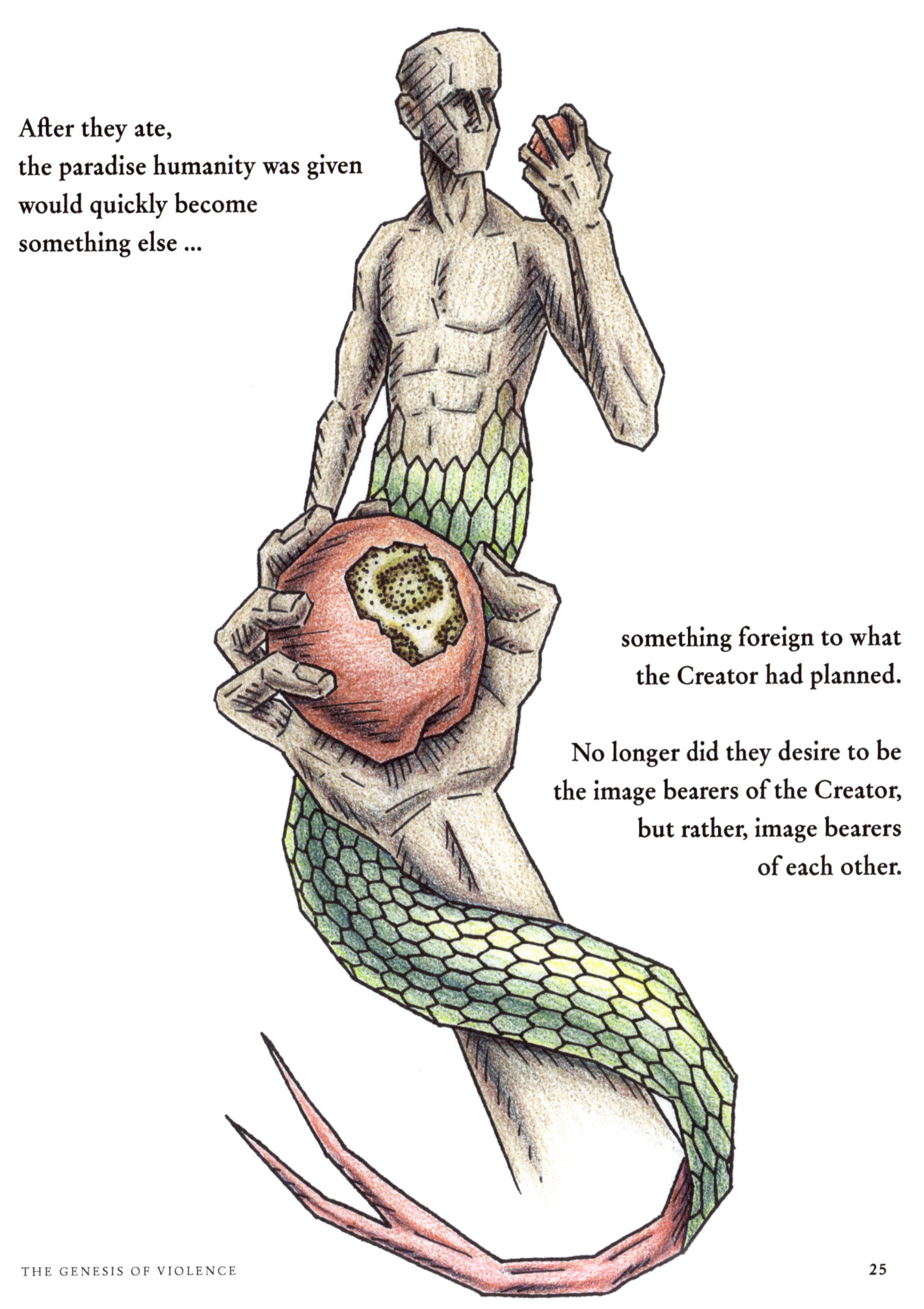

something foreign to what
the Creator had planned.

No longer did they desire to be
the image bearers of the Creator,
but rather, image bearers
of each other.

THE GENESIS OF VIOLENCE

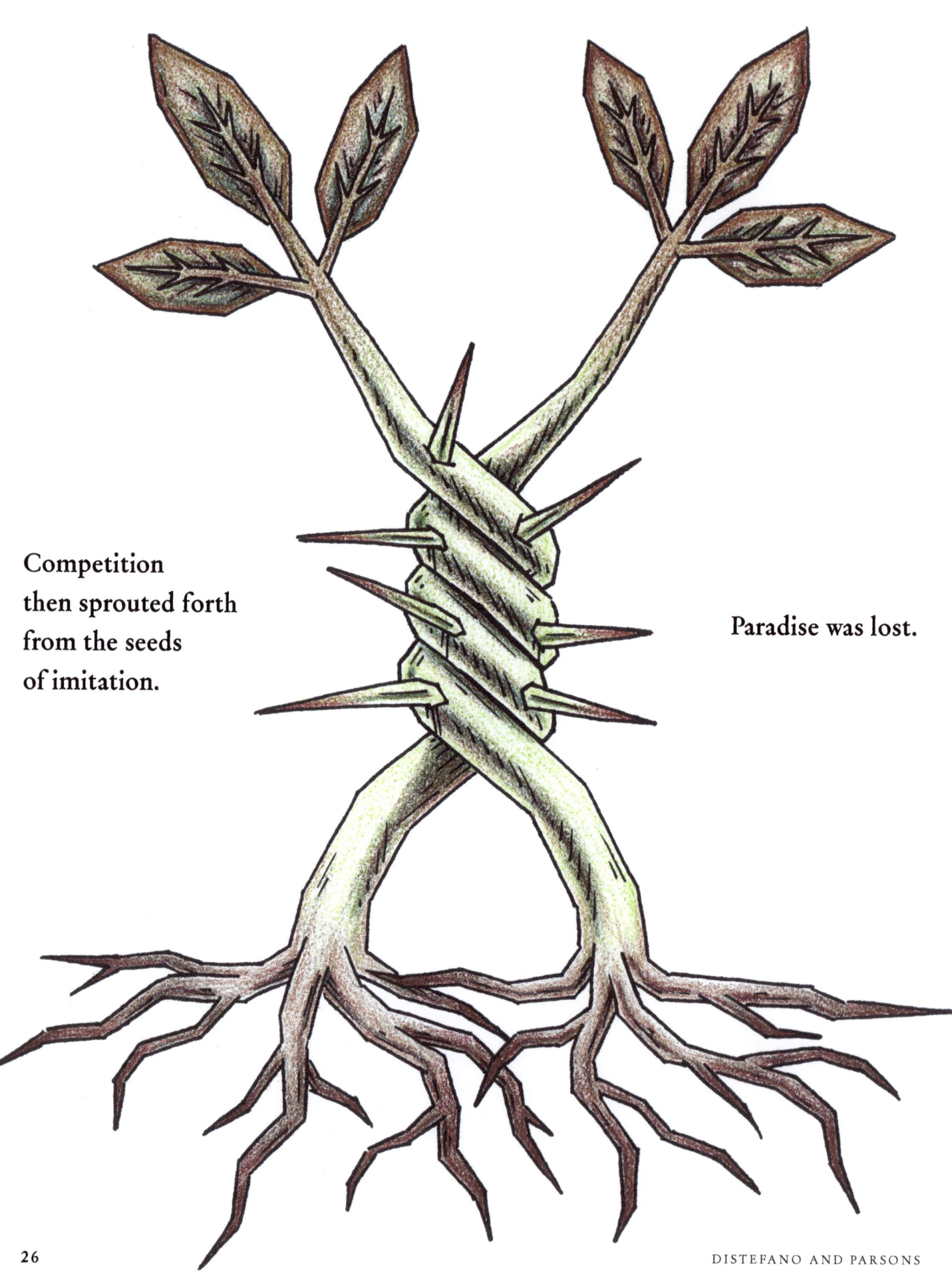

Competition then sprouted forth from the seeds of imitation.

Paradise was lost.

CHAPTER II

Blood and Sacrifice

Now, there arose a tale of two brothers, Cain and Abel. In an attempt to earn the favor of the Creator, the brothers made offerings.

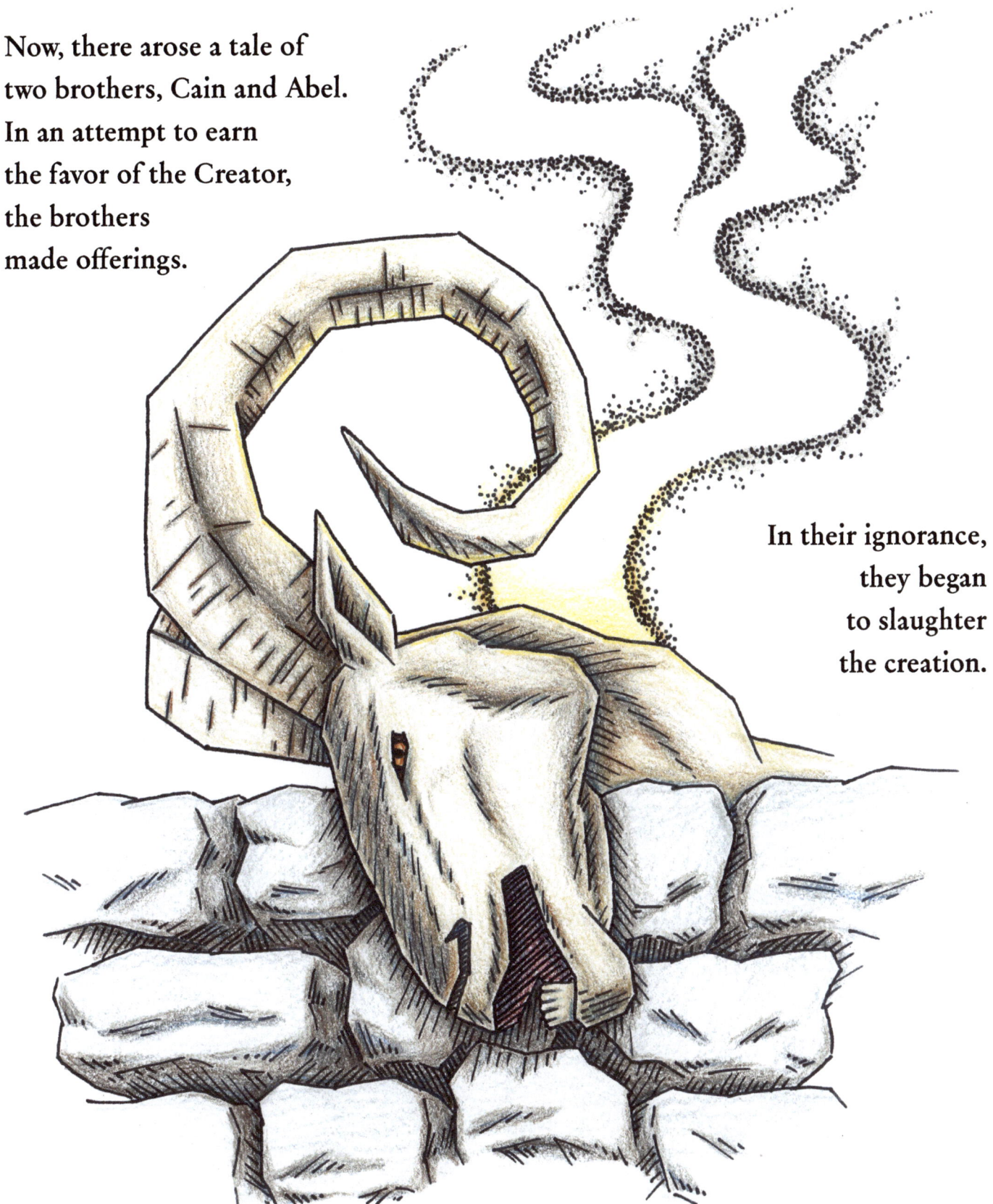

In their ignorance, they began to slaughter the creation.

On blood-soaked altars they offered to the gods of their own mind whole hosts of rams, bulls, and lambs.

THE GENESIS OF VIOLENCE

Believing the Creator
had favor for Abel's offering,
Cain then rose up
against Abel
and murdered him.

For the first time,
human blood was spilled.
Brother against brother,
flesh against flesh.

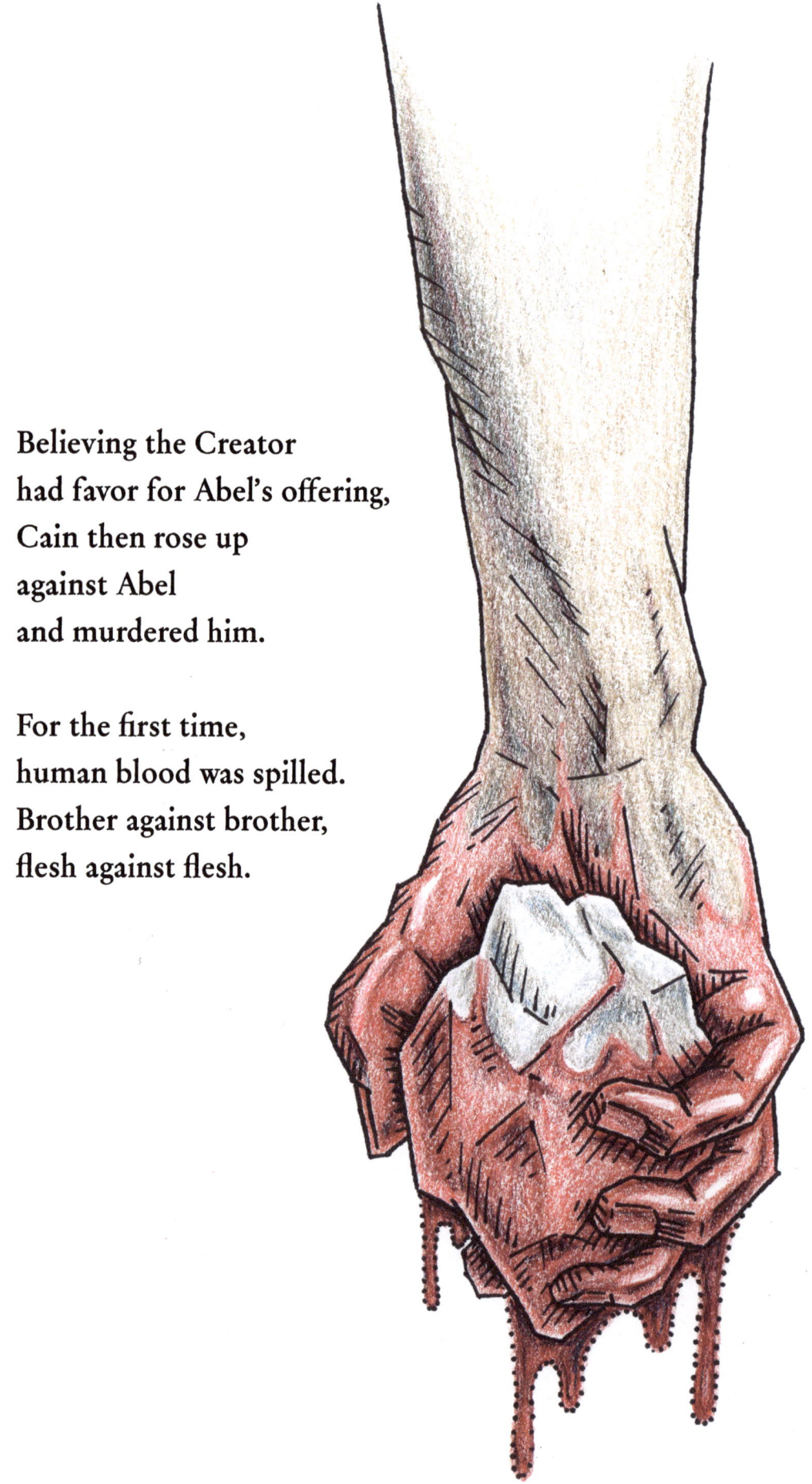

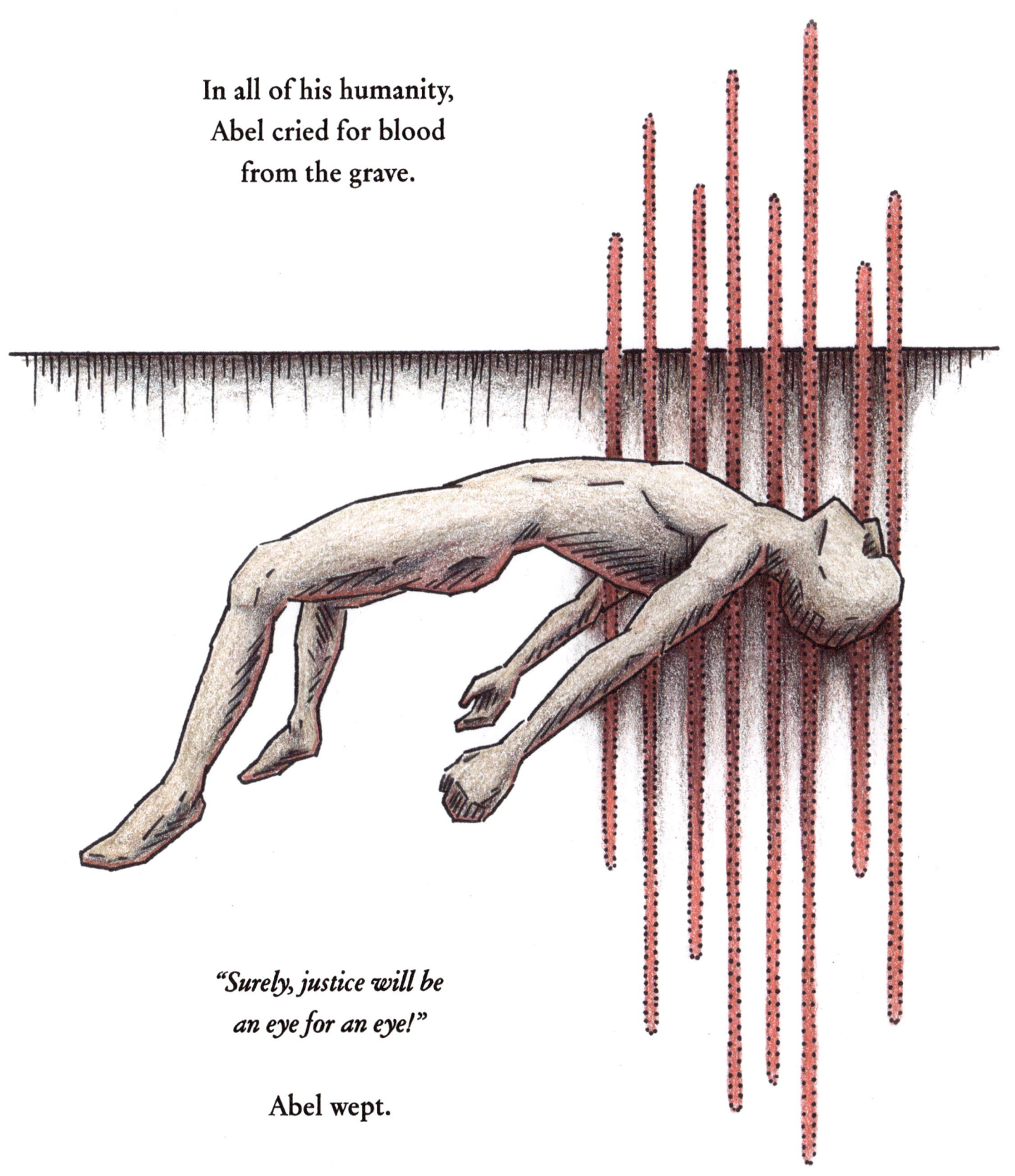

In all of his humanity, Abel cried for blood from the grave.

"Surely, justice will be an eye for an eye!"

Abel wept.

THE GENESIS OF VIOLENCE

However,
the Creator
would take
no
such
vengeance.

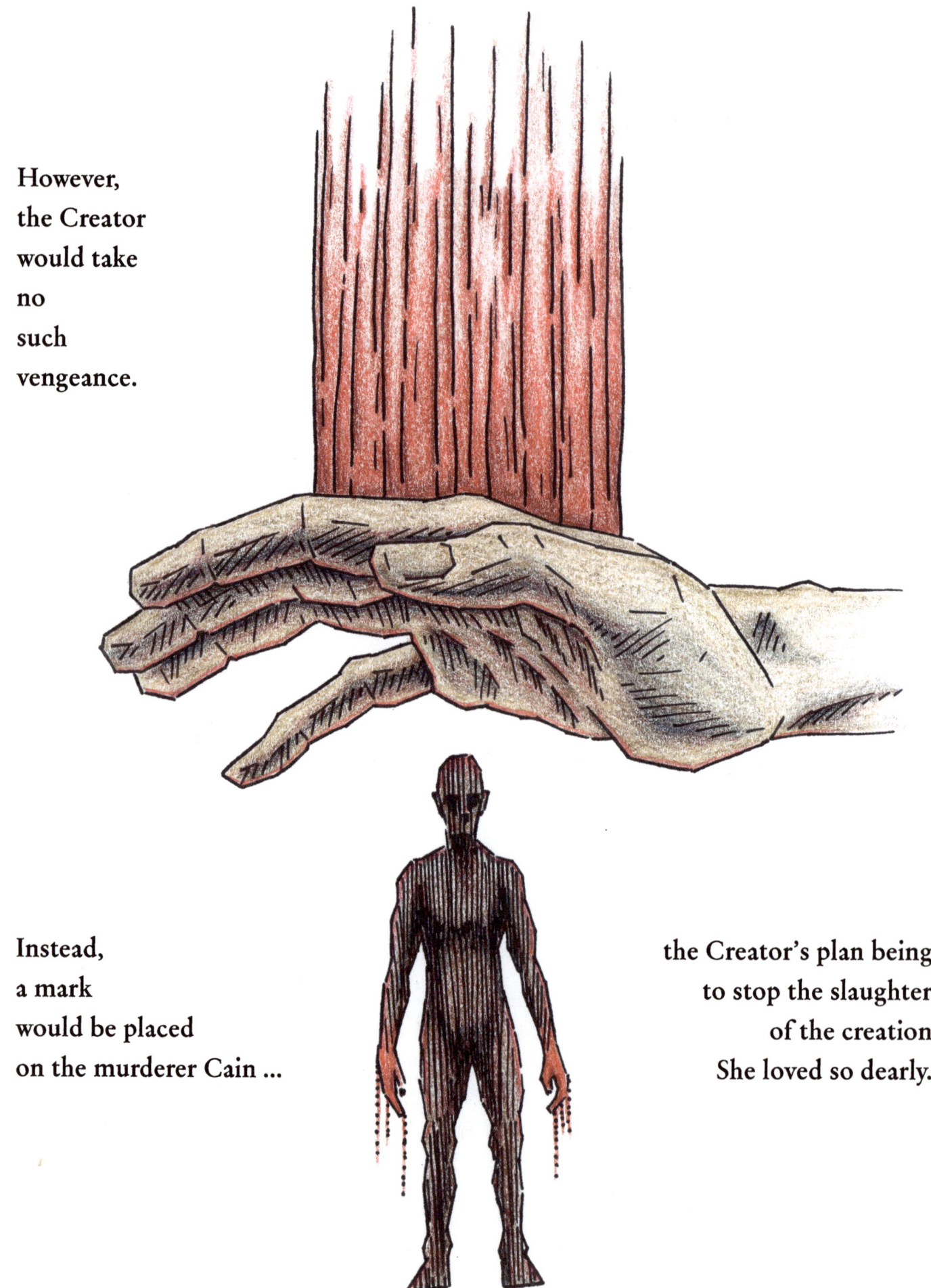

Instead,
a mark
would be placed
on the murderer Cain ...

the Creator's plan being
to stop the slaughter
of the creation
She loved so dearly.

But it would be in vain
as just a few short generations later,

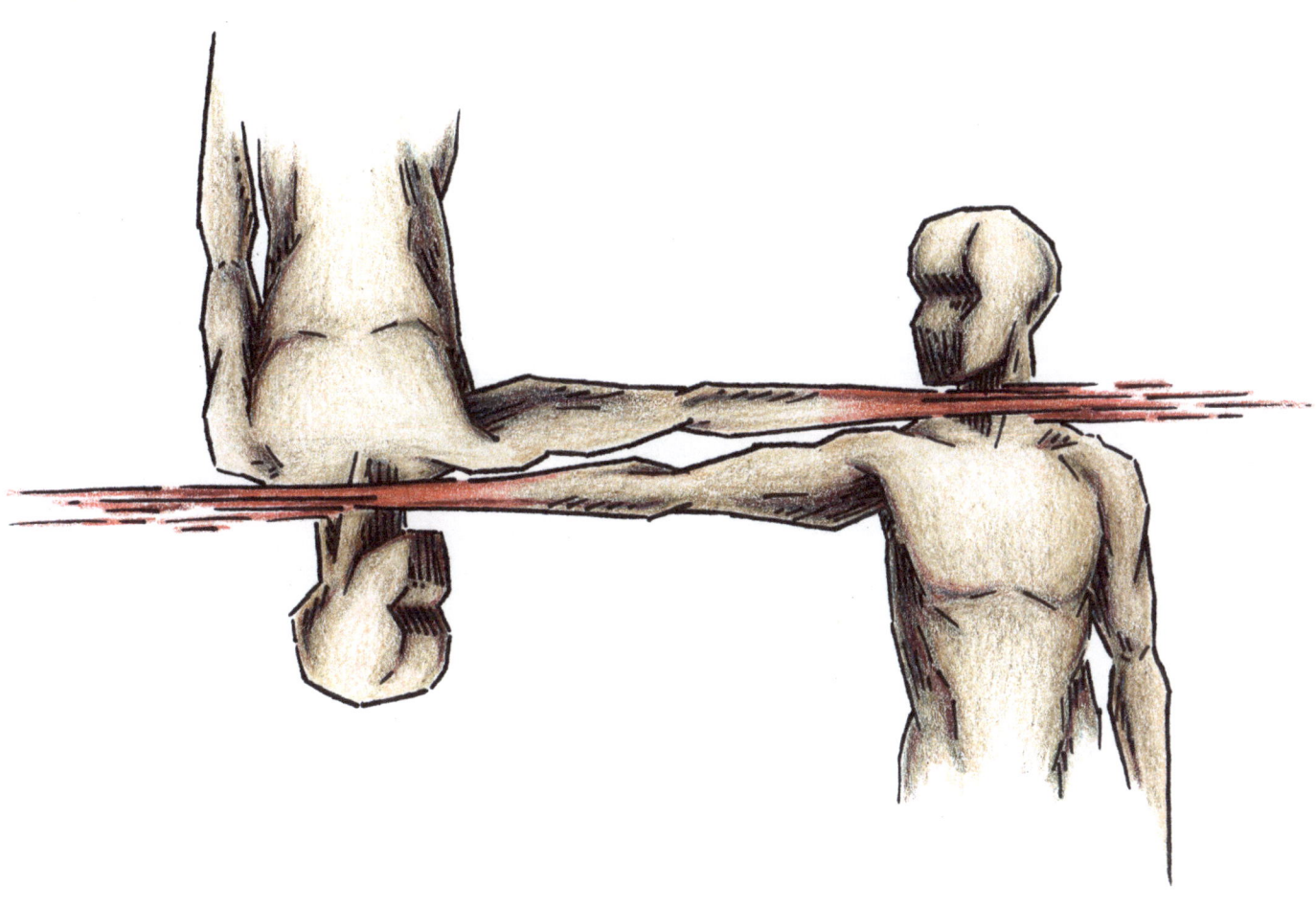

retributive violence
would grip humanity.

Within the walls of the first city,

madness ensued ...   Everywhere ...
  violence ...   all the time ...
    mayhem ...   everything ...

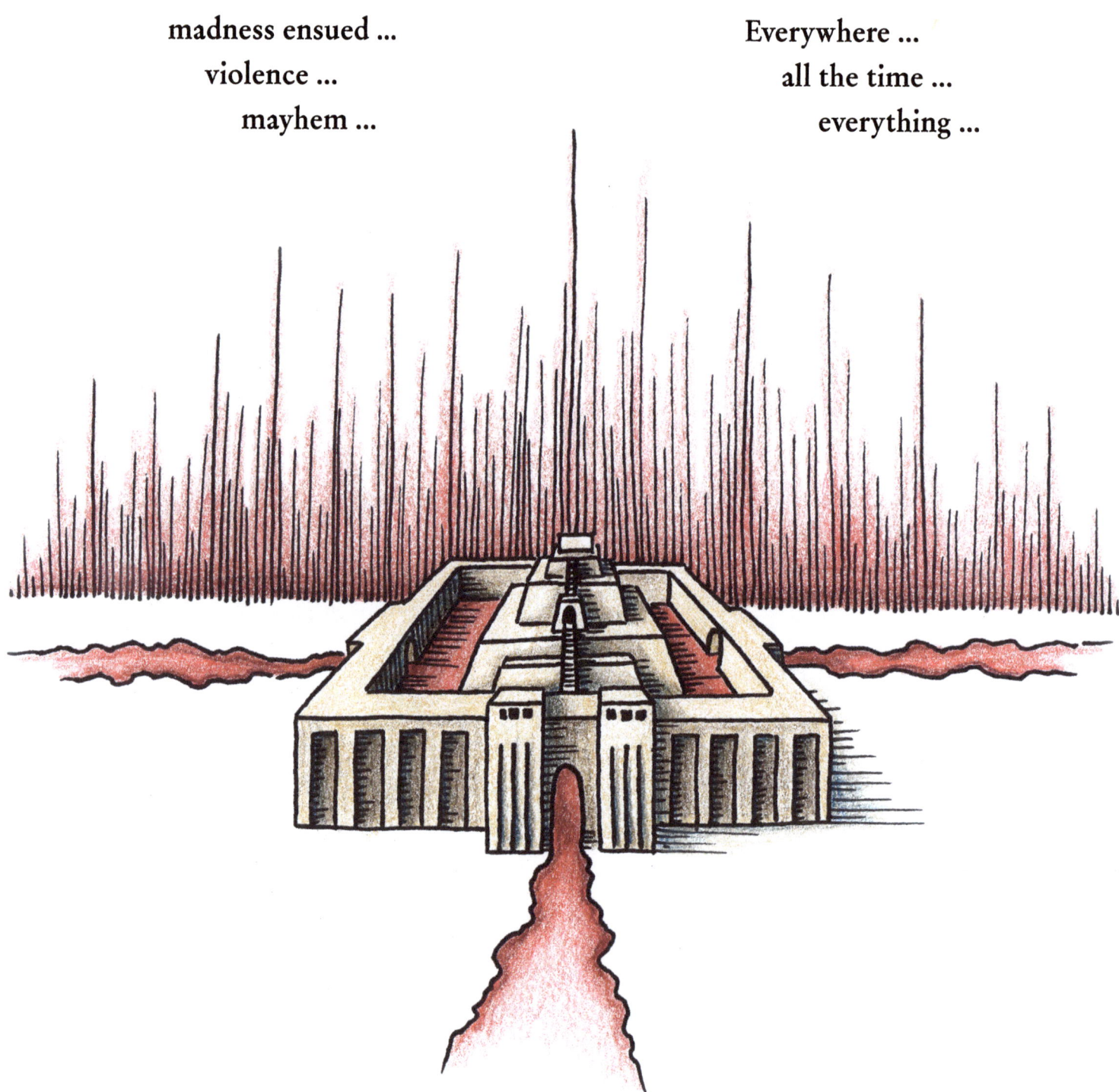

Wound a man and he would surely put you to death.
Men, women, children ...
all of them!

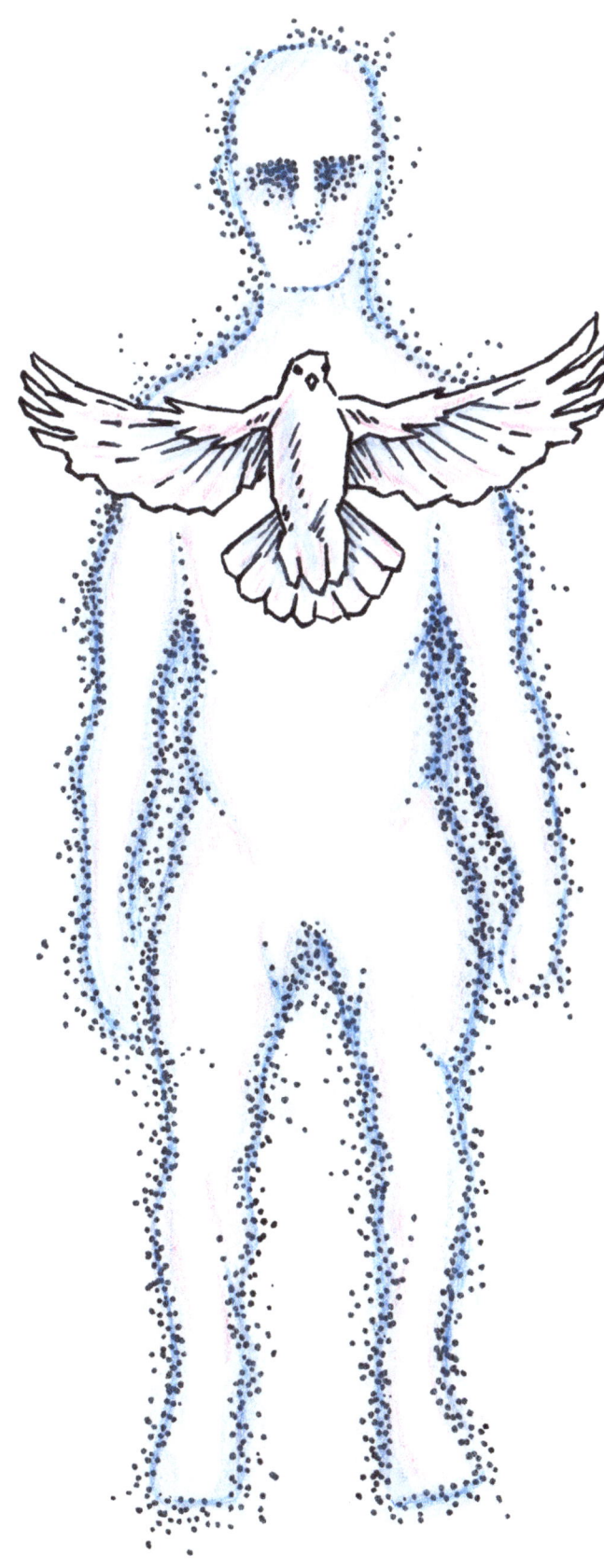

But there was one
who would not engage
in the brutality.

In the midst of the terror,
Noah and his family
found favor
in the Creator's eyes
by refusing to return
violence with violence.

This was a man of peace,
a man whom the Creator
hoped would remain true
to the divine image he bore.

As the violence surrounding Noah began to engulf humanity
like a powerful flood,
he and his family trusted the Creator to guide them through

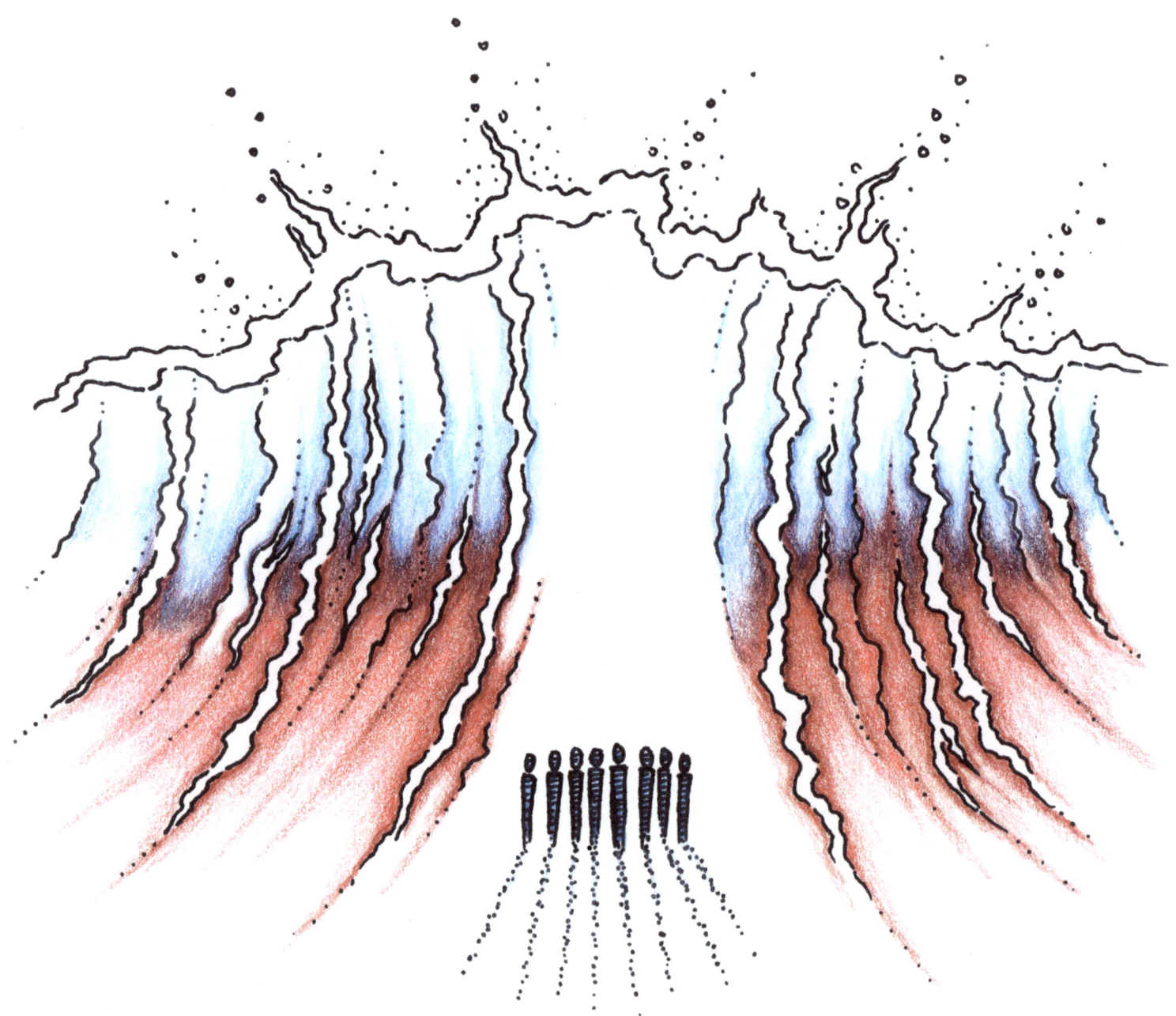

And so, they were graciously spared from the destruction.
After a time, they were all that remained.

So, there remained hope for a peaceful future, a better life.

THE GENESIS OF VIOLENCE

But hope was short lived.

To give thanks to the Creator,
Noah, in all his righteous ignorance,
did what humanity could not help but do ...
sacrifice the creation.

Blame,
scapegoat,
accuse.

Sadly, this again would move them
toward yet another cycle of violence.

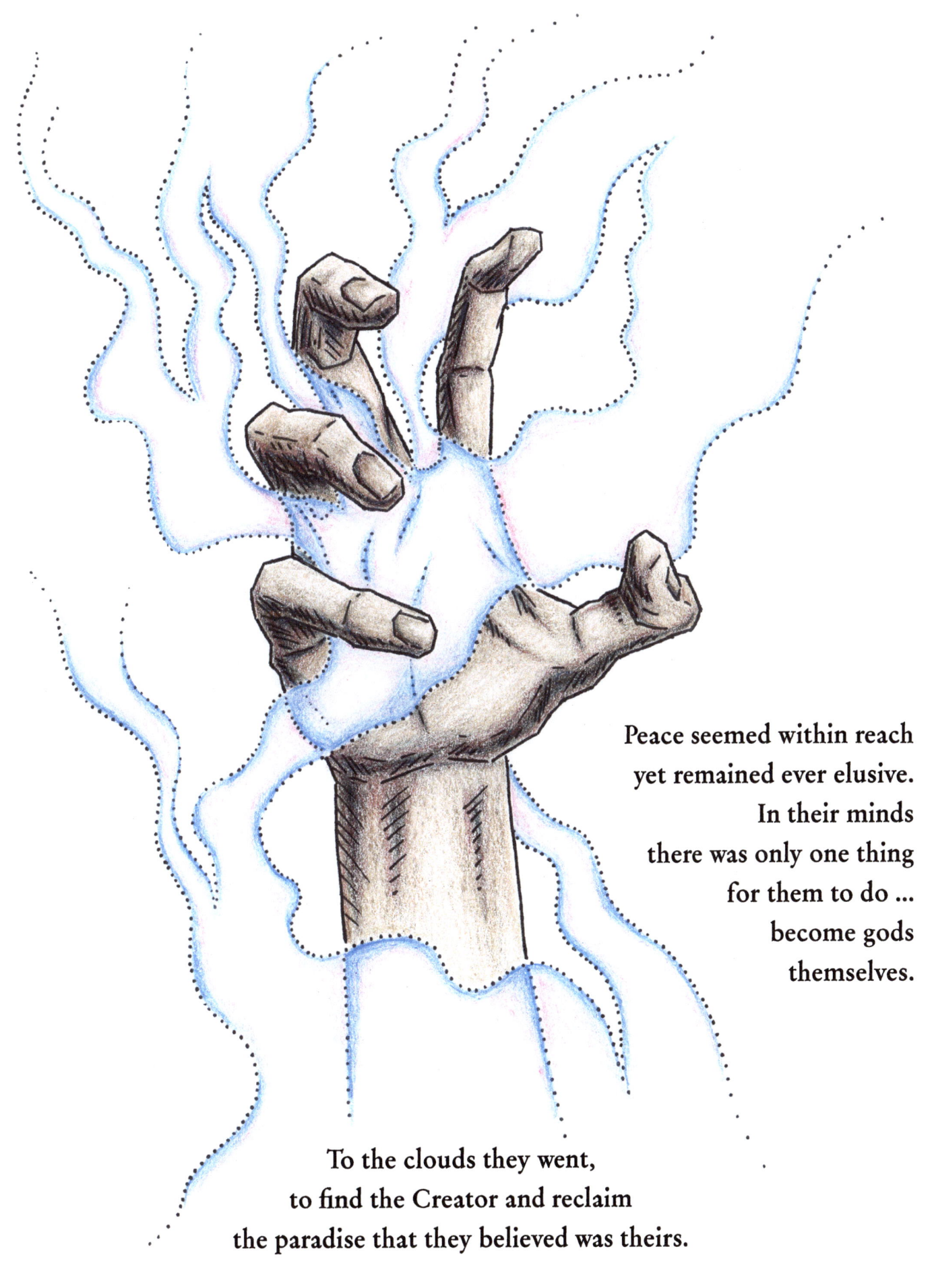

Peace seemed within reach yet remained ever elusive. In their minds there was only one thing for them to do ... become gods themselves.

To the clouds they went, to find the Creator and reclaim the paradise that they believed was theirs.

With bricks and tar,
stones and mortar,
a ziggurat was built.

At the top,
a great altar stood,
and it gleefully accepted
countless human lives.

To the gods
of their own imagination,
humanity offered
more and more
precious blood
in hopes
that they would again
be made whole.

This caused the Creator great grief.

The creation had gone so wrong.
So, to save them from themselves, the Creator scattered humanity.
This way, the great altar that so willingly accepted so much flesh might tumble down.
Perhaps, somehow, humanity could then begin to listen to the Creator's voice.
If they were to ever return to a place of paradise, they would have to.

Chapter III

The Call of the Patriarch

After a time,
humanity began to settle
throughout all the earth.

Cities were established,
empires born.

Various religions took shape,
with sacrifice
being the lifeblood of them all.

To the gods
of their imagination,
humanity slew the creation,
the greatest of all sacrifices
being the firstborn child.

THE GENESIS OF VIOLENCE

Over and over,
humanity offered their sons—
indeed, even their precious daughters—
on countless blood-soaked altars ...

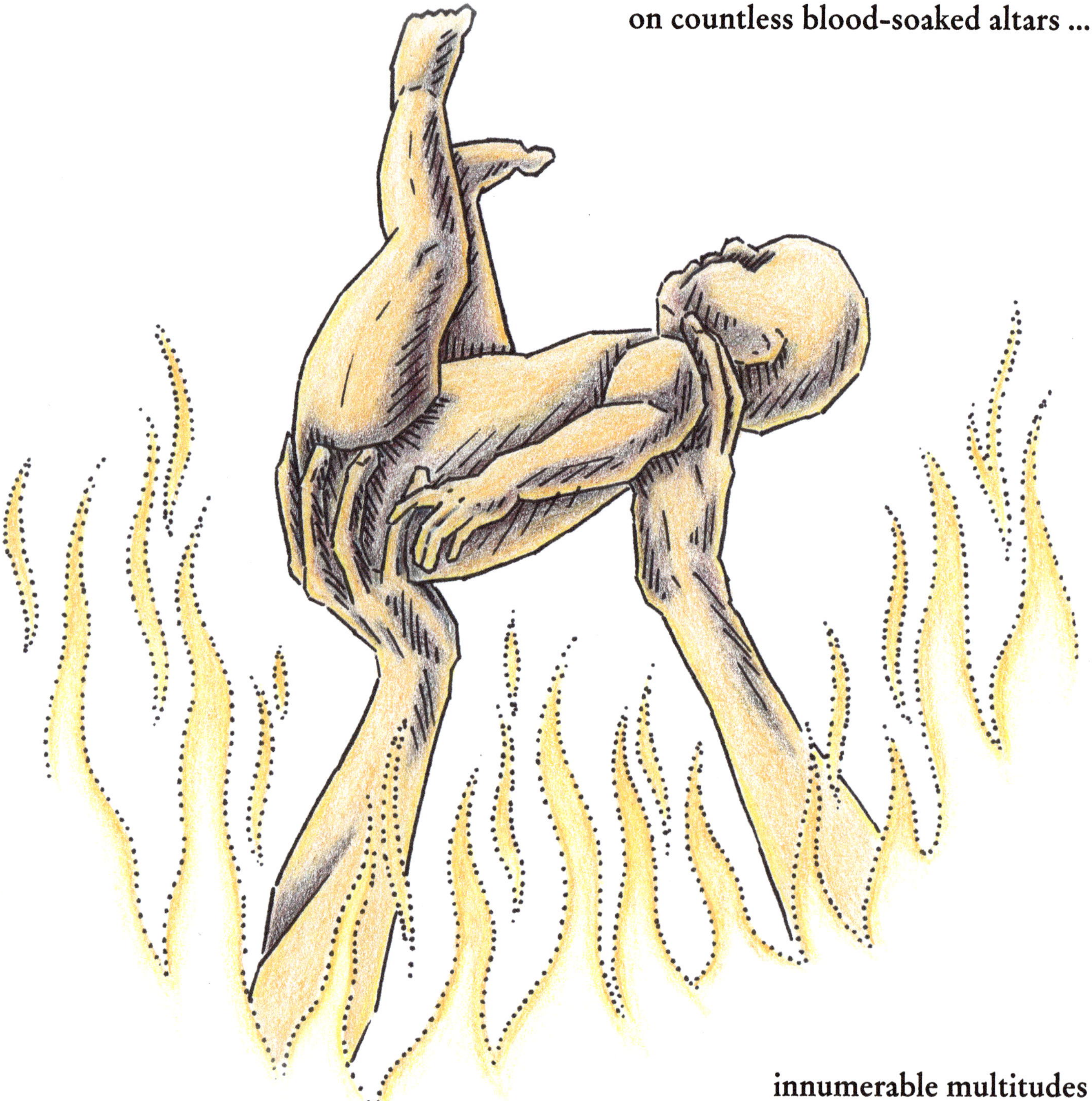

innumerable multitudes
of their beautiful children.

Throat after throat,
brutally slit
in an attempt to appease gods
that were nothing
but mere inventions
of the mind.

Altars to lifeless deities
again rose up
and became the centers
of civilization,
culture,
and religion.

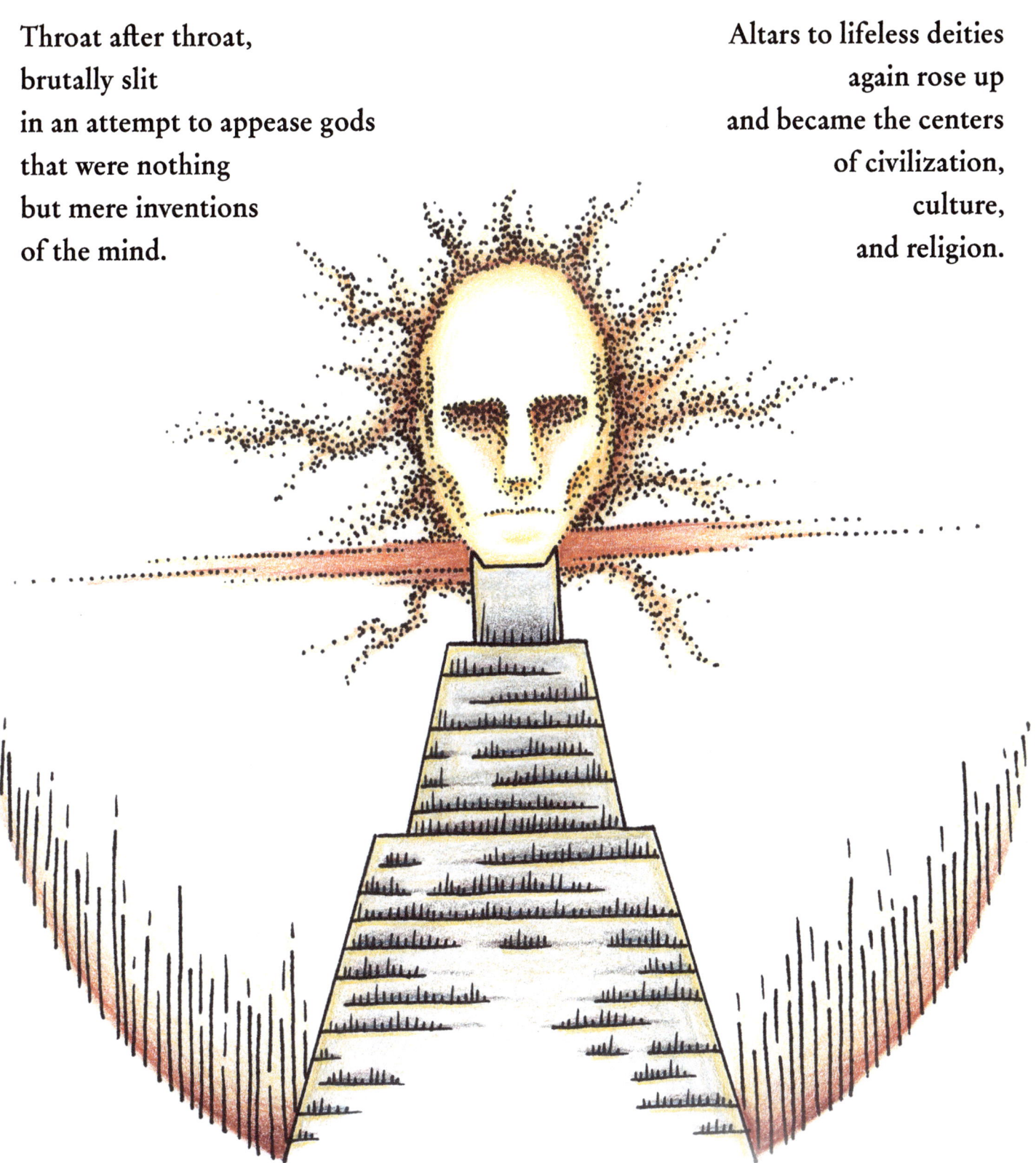

Humanity trudged along with perplexing vainness.
She truly had forgotten whose image she bore.

THE GENESIS OF VIOLENCE

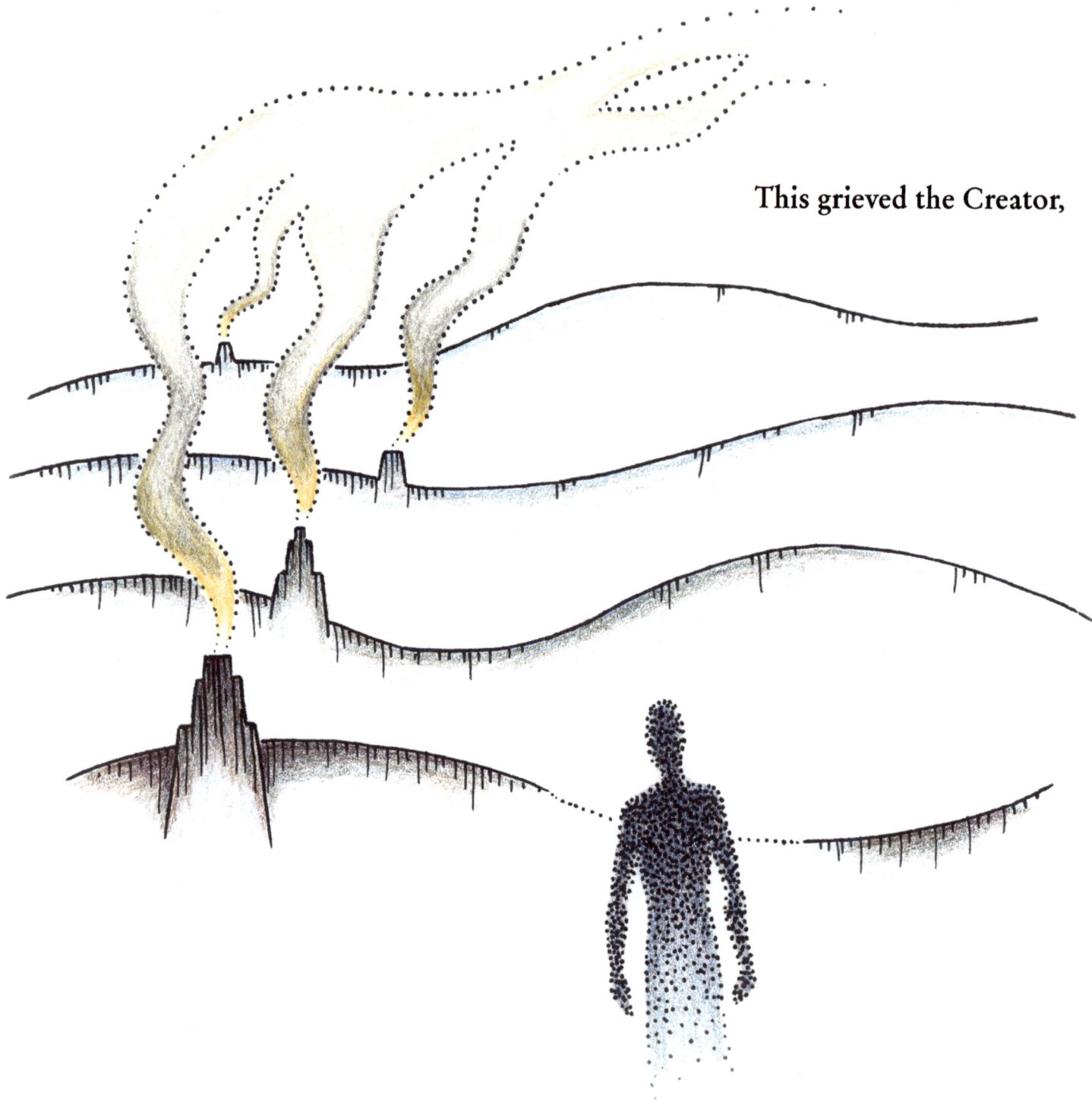

This grieved the Creator,

so to again alter the course of humanity's history,
one man would have to be called upon.
He would have to listen to the voice of the Creator
and lead his people away from the practices
they so eagerly engaged in.

His name was Abraham,
and he was,
in a sense,
to become the patriarch
of humanity.

This man, Abraham, while a ripe old age,
had a son named Isaac, whom he loved,
but who would one day inevitably be the next sacrifice to the gods.

And so, once Isaac became of age, Abraham,
like every one of his contemporaries before him,
saddled up his donkey and made the journey
to the place where he would slay his son.

THE GENESIS OF VIOLENCE

While on the way, Abraham looked to the sky
and thought he heard a voice ...

*"... Spill the blood of your son Isaac
and burn the body,
for I desire the smell of flesh!
To the mountain in the region of Moriah
you shall go ..."*

So, Abraham went.

When Abraham reached Moriah, he bound Isaac's hands and placed him on the sacred altar that he had prepared beforehand.

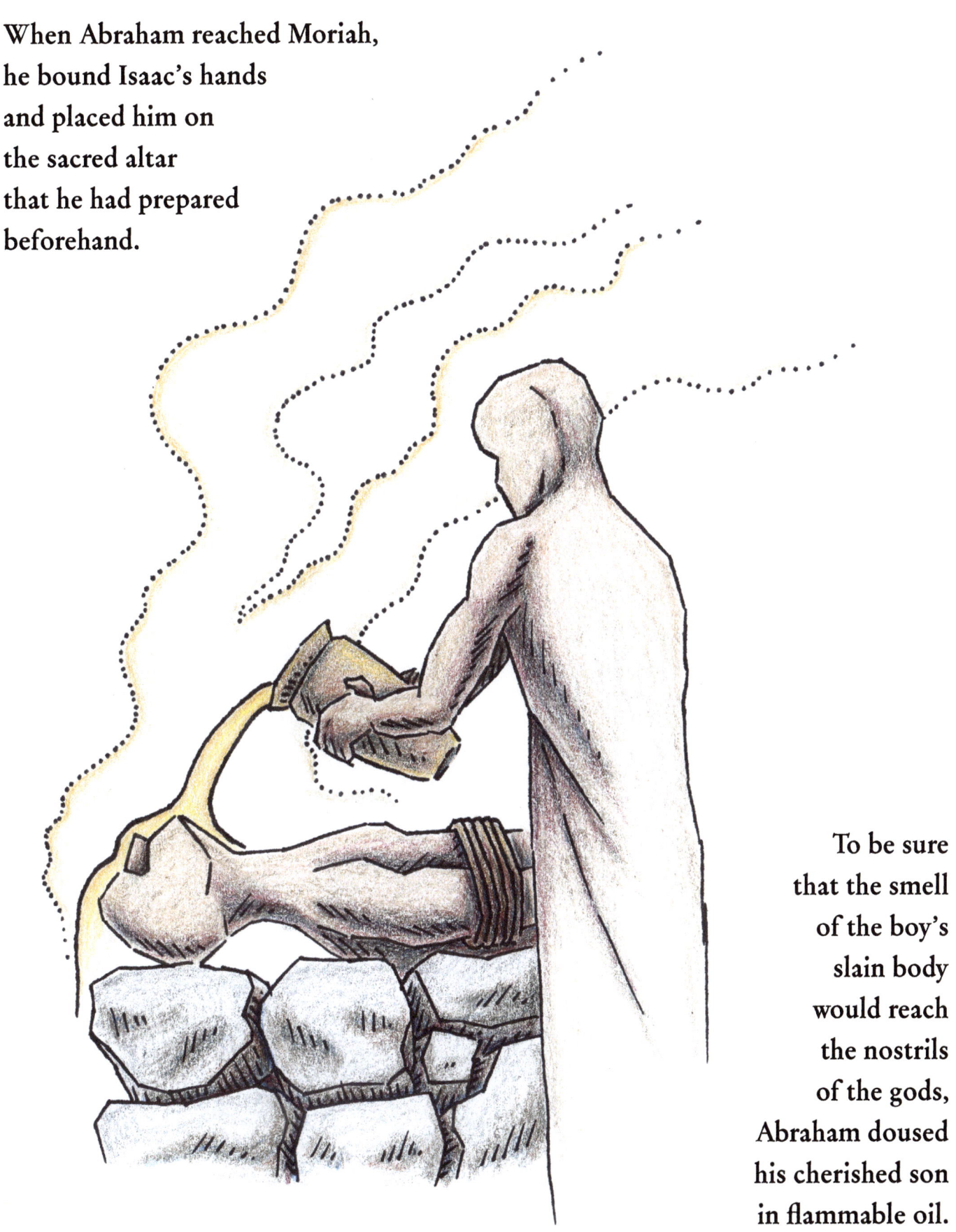

To be sure that the smell of the boy's slain body would reach the nostrils of the gods, Abraham doused his cherished son in flammable oil.

THE GENESIS OF VIOLENCE

Then Abraham grabbed the sharpest of knives
so the slaying would be quick.

With the smell of oil in the air
and the look of horror on Isaac's beautiful face,
Abraham went to sever his son's throat
so that his warm blood could cover
the stone altar he lay upon.

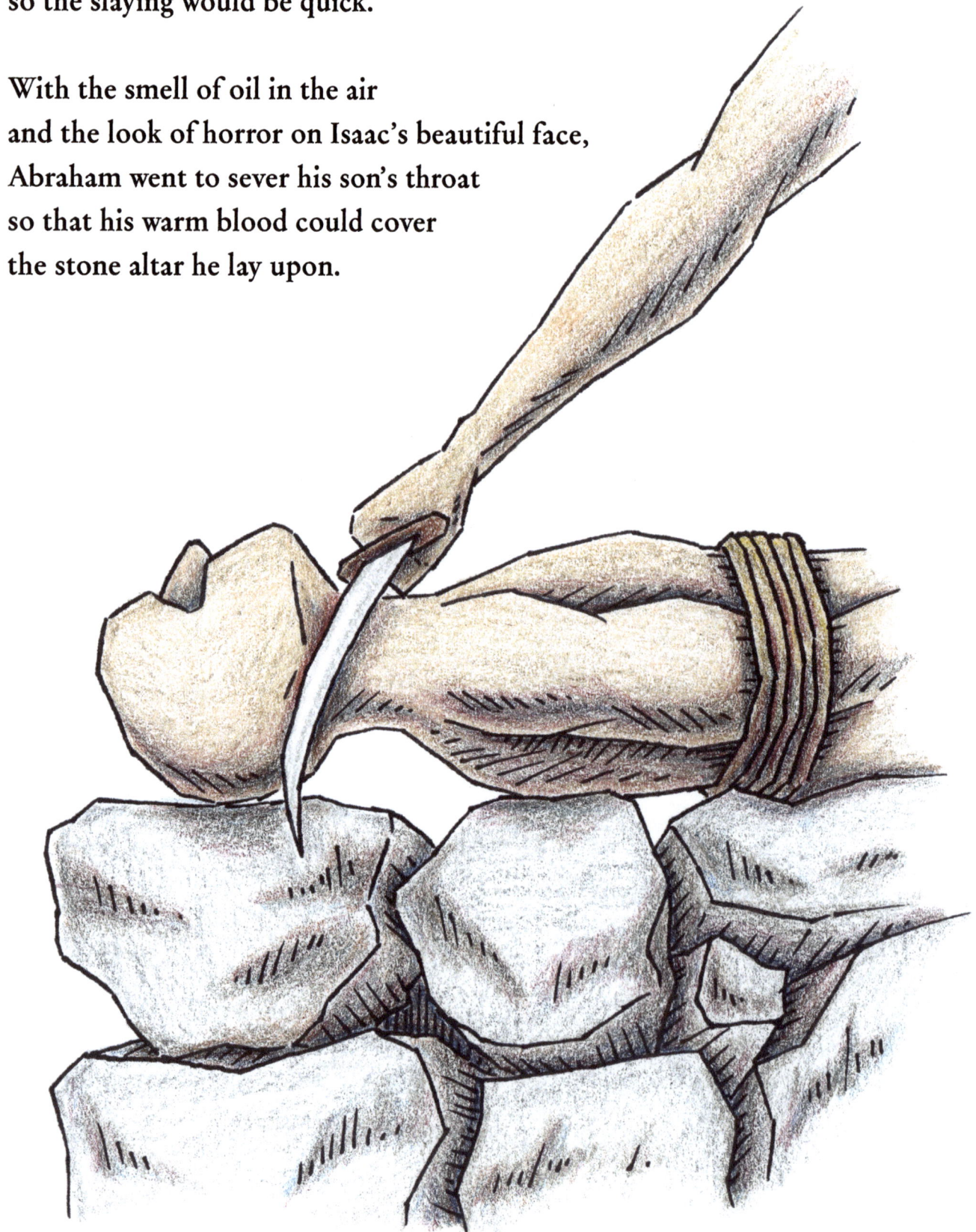

But suddenly,
and almost out of nowhere,
an angel sent by the Creator
called loudly to Abraham
and commanded him to halt.

*"Abraham! Abraham!
Do not lay a hand on the boy!"*

So, Abraham, with his hands still shaking and with sweat pouring down his brow, took heed of the command and fell to his knees,

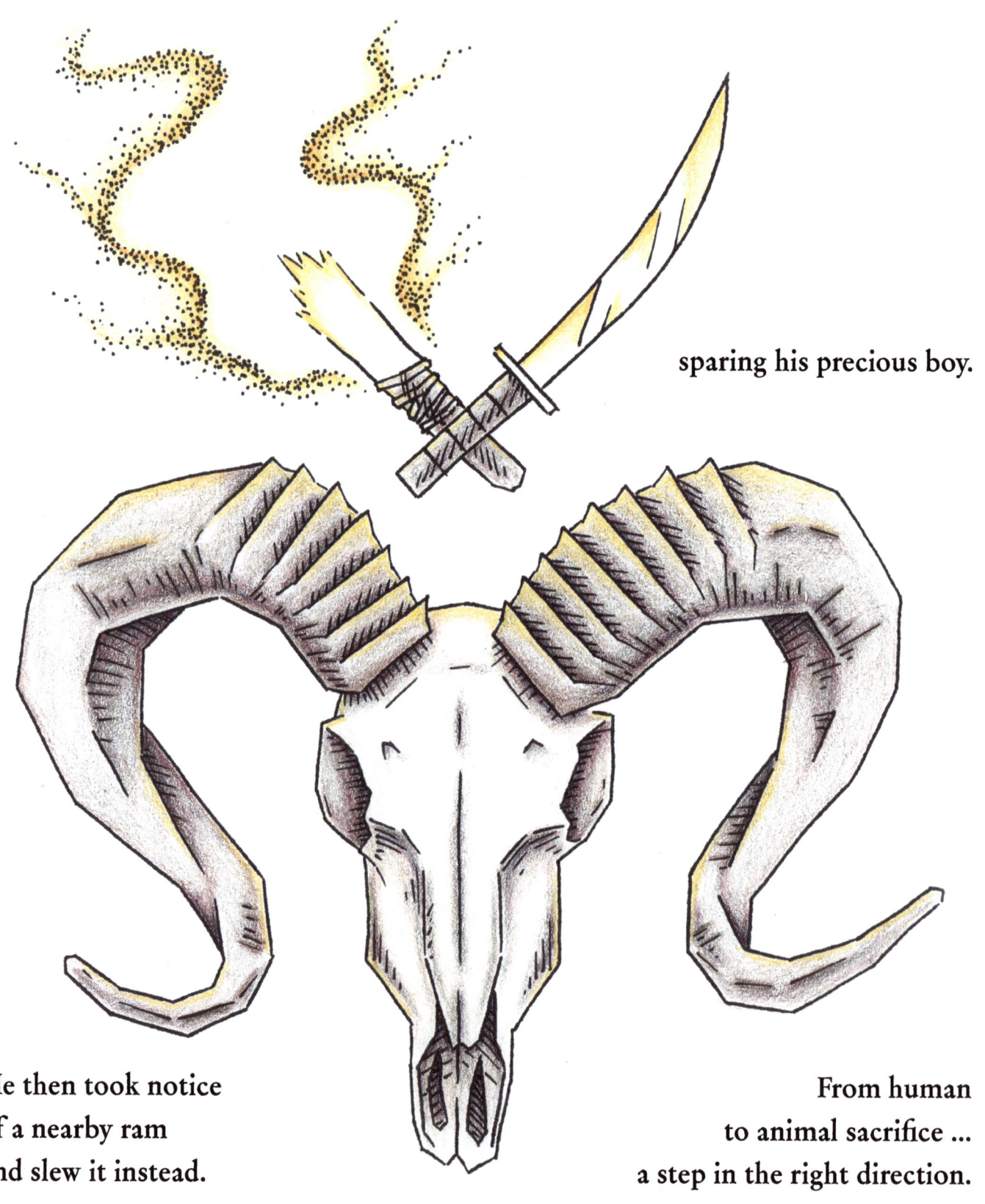

sparing his precious boy.

He then took notice of a nearby ram and slew it instead.

From human to animal sacrifice ... a step in the right direction.

Progress had been made because of this one act, and this pleased the Creator, who saw that it was good.

But there was still work to be done.

THE GENESIS OF VIOLENCE

55

CHAPTER IV

Sibling Rivalry

Well after Abraham's passing,
Isaac married and bore two sons,
Esau and Jacob.

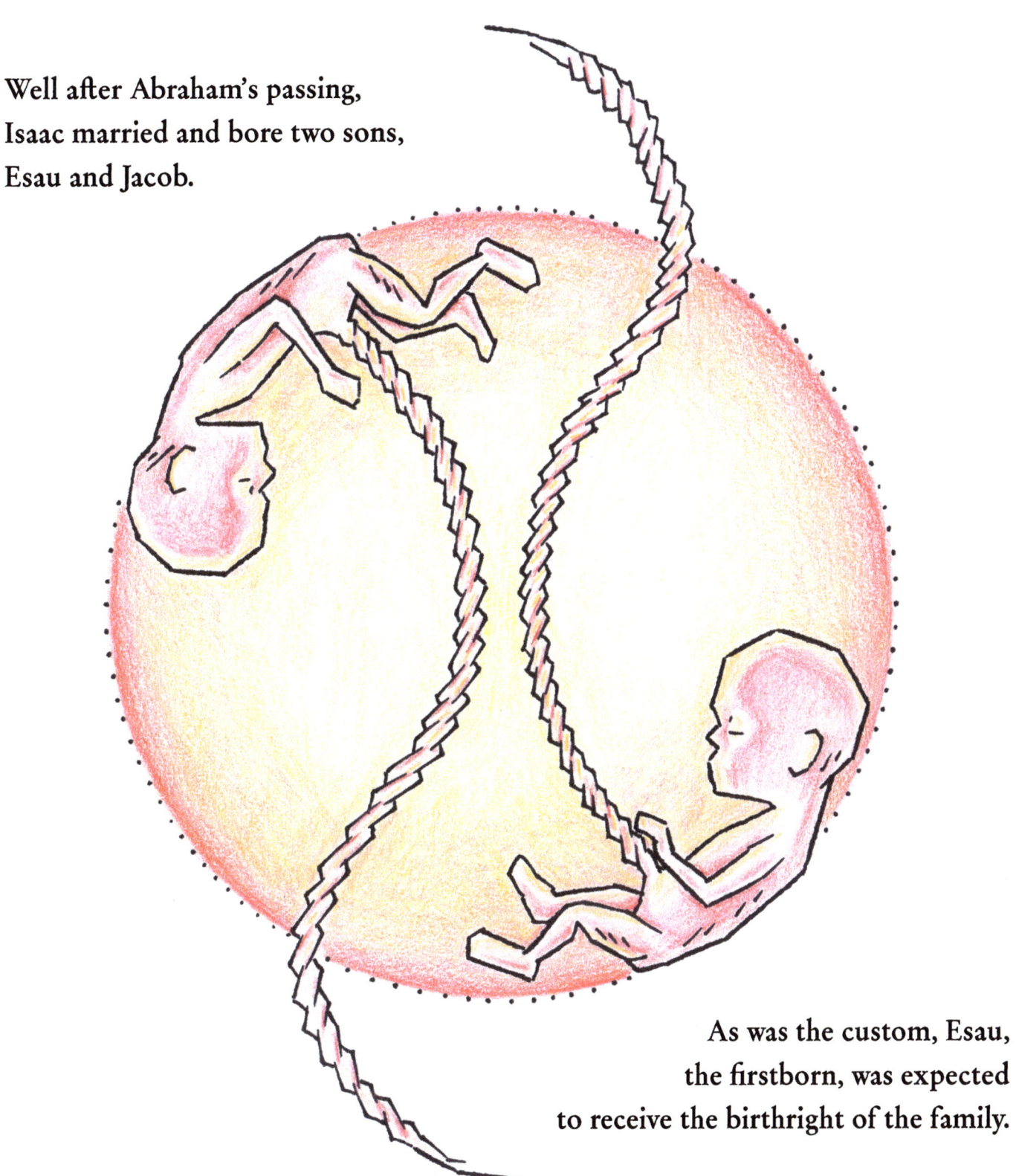

As was the custom, Esau,
the firstborn, was expected
to receive the birthright of the family.

However, this family was going to be different.
In this family, the youngest
would be served by the eldest.

THE GENESIS OF VIOLENCE

59

This caused a deep seeded rivalry which, unsurprisingly, again led brother to rise up against brother.

Sides were taken, lines were drawn in the sand. And a family with so much potential again teetered on the edge of ruin.

Jacob, the younger brother,
was deceptive,

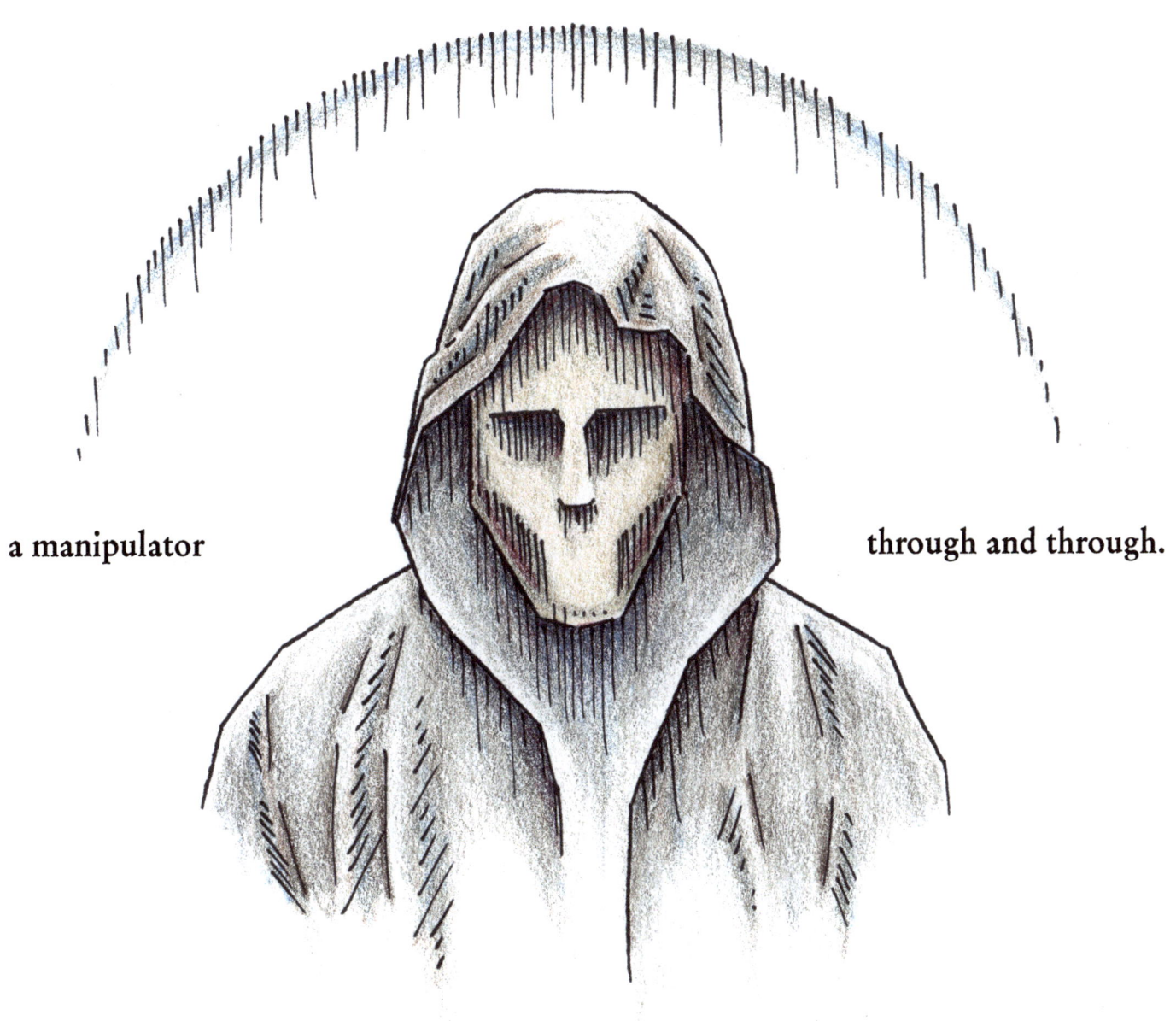

a manipulator   through and through.

He was favored by his mother.

Esau, on the other hand,
was impulsive and capricious.

His father showed him great favor.

On two separate occasions, the crafty Jacob deceived Esau, which led him to gain

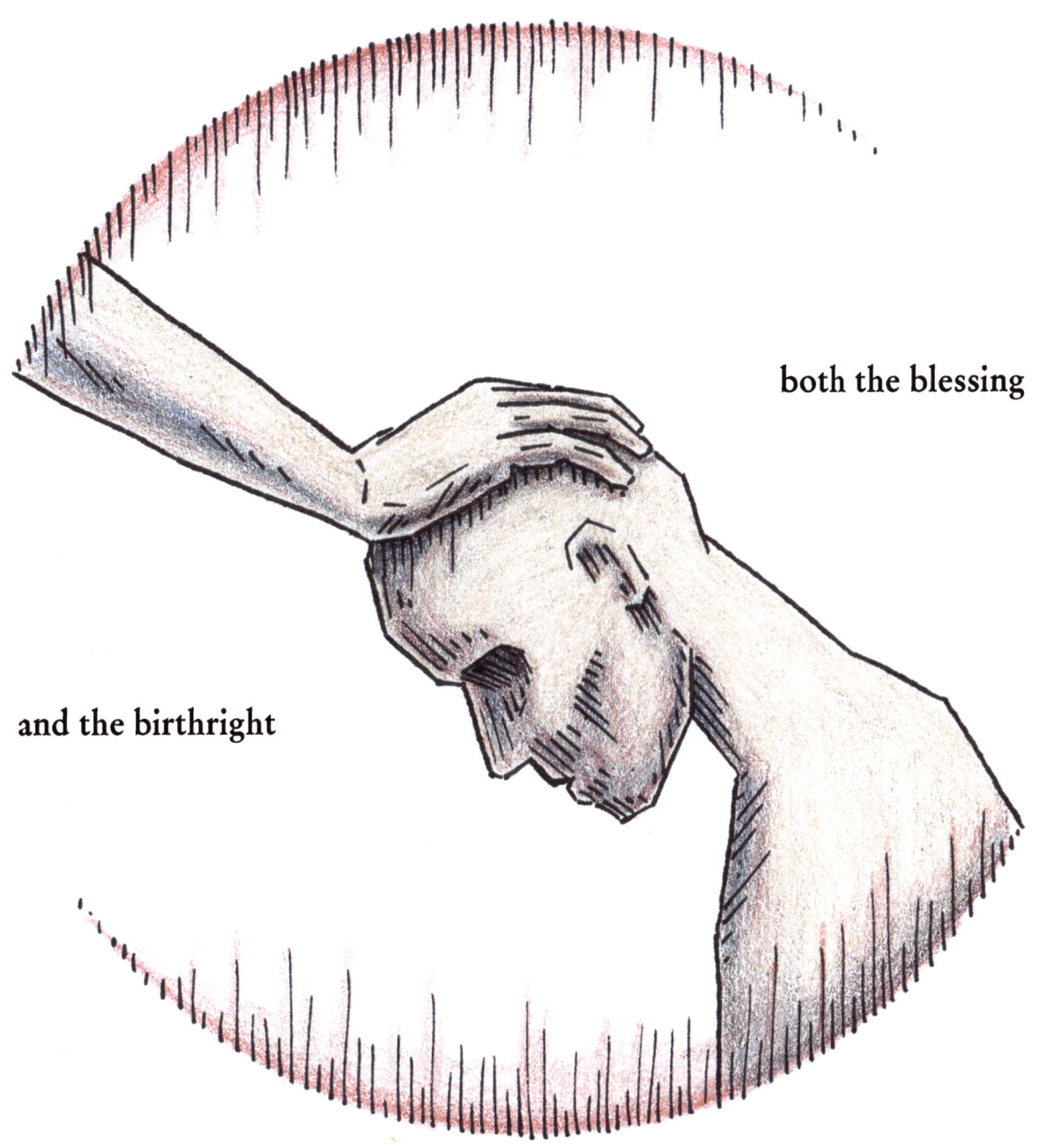

both the blessing

and the birthright

that was supposed to belong to the eldest son.

Rather predictably, this led to hostility and violence, as Esau would not take too kindly to Jacob's scheming.

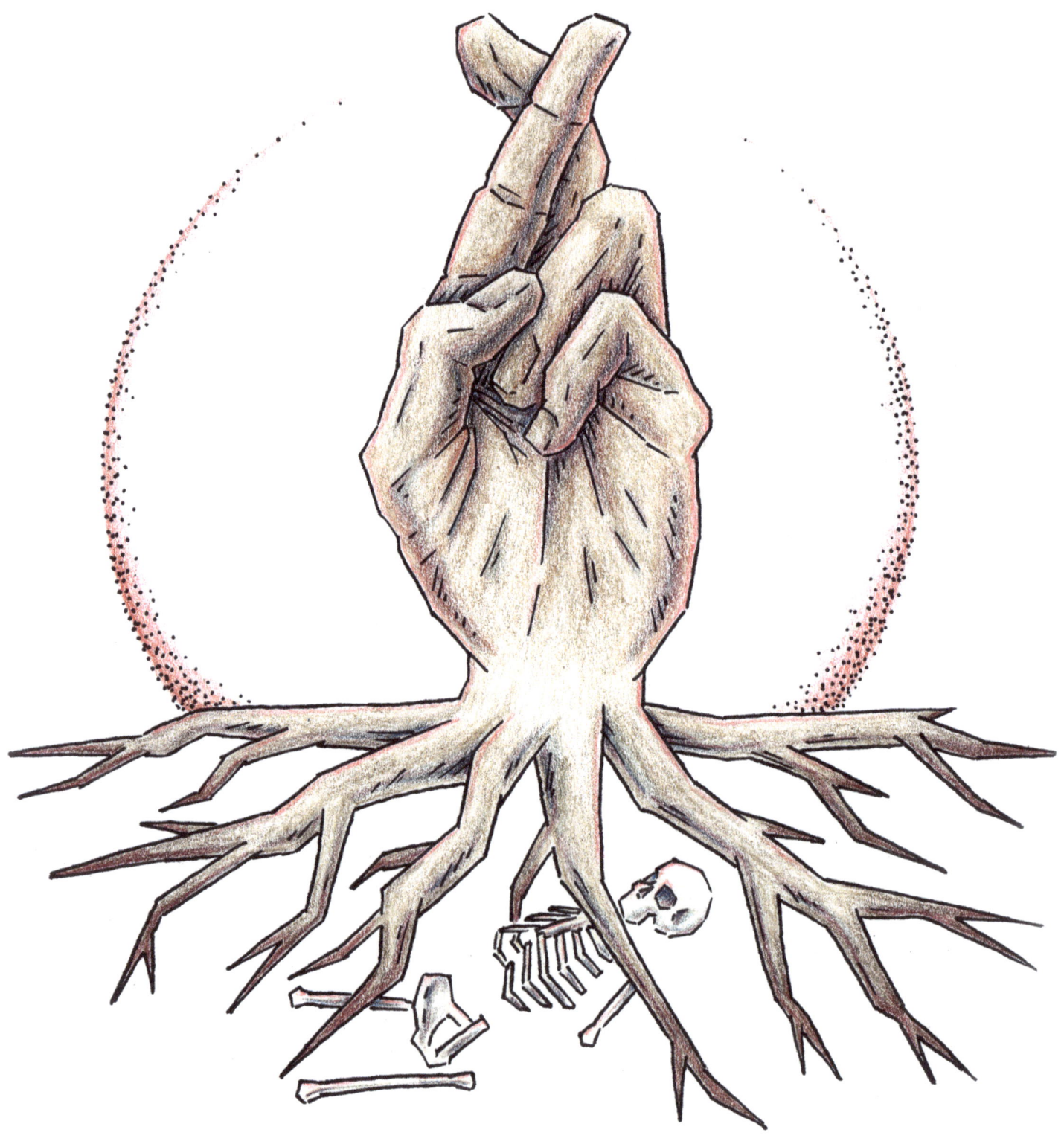

An eye for an eye,

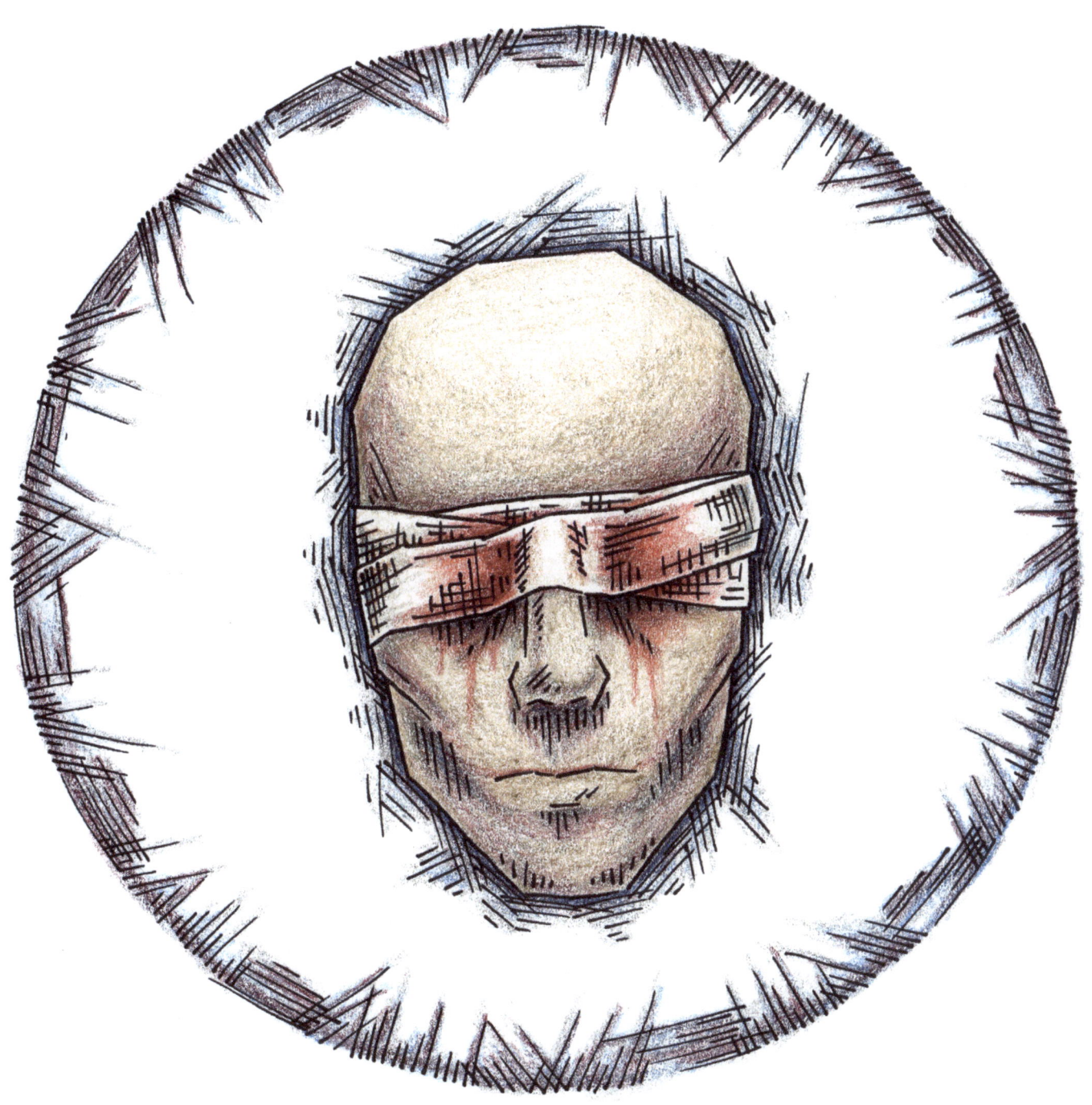

the justice of humanity.

Yet, in spite of Esau's vow to kill his younger brother,
Jacob, with his mother's help, was able to narrowly escape with his life.

This exile, however, would come at a cost,
leading Jacob to become a mere servant of a relative named Laban,
who was quite shrewd himself.

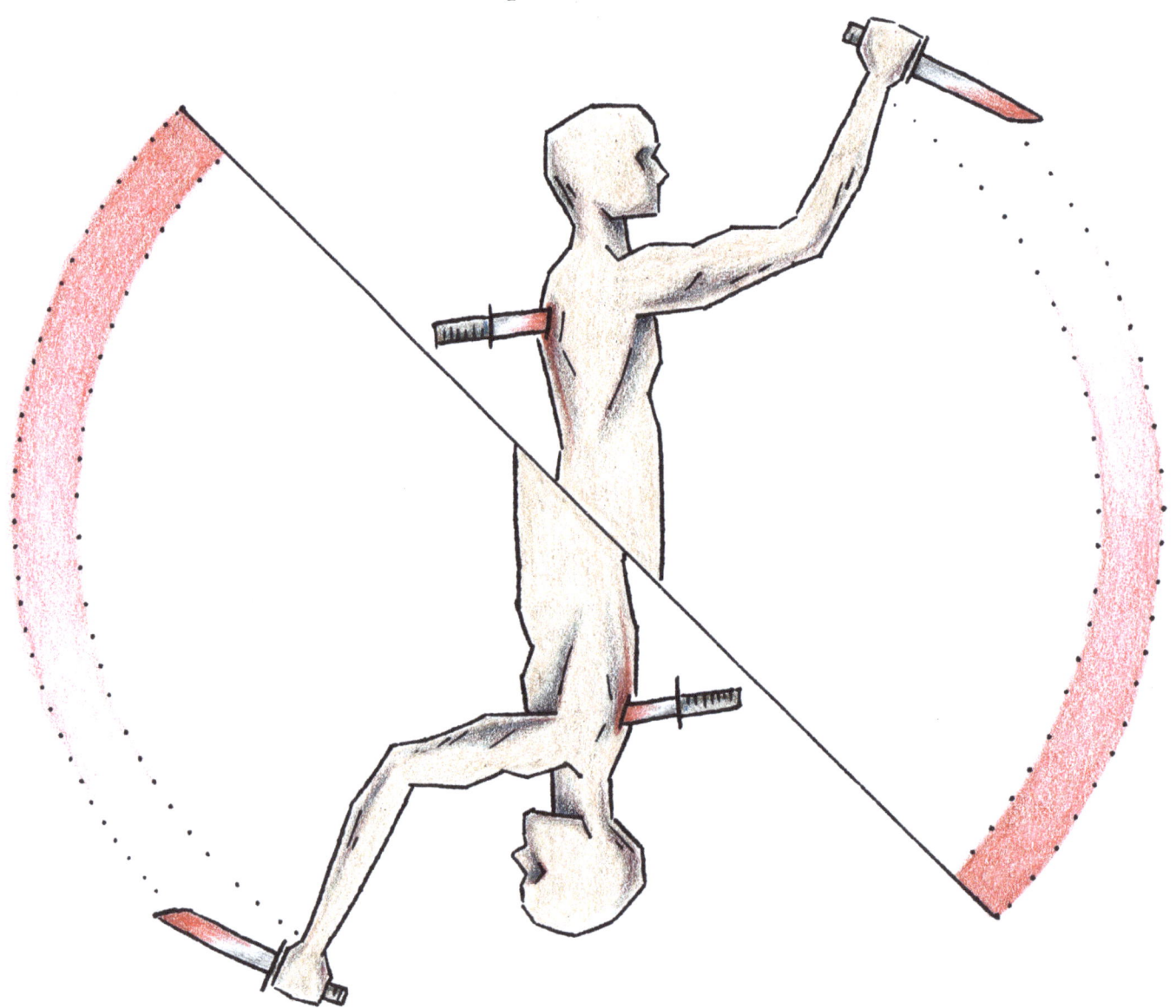

On numerous occasions throughout their relationship,
the two engaged in acts of cunning that led to envy and strife.

Indeed, they were nearly mirror images of one another.

Because of the contentious situation Jacob found himself in,
he was again forced to flee his home.

But this time,
Laban hotly pursued,
and quickly caught up with the escapee.

Soon enough, there they were,
face to face, toe to toe,
with bloodlust in their eyes.

But then, in what could only be explained as divine intervention,
the two dropped their guard and made a covenant to not harm one another.

For that day, at least, peace would reign.

THE GENESIS OF VIOLENCE

Continuing in the spirit of peace and understanding, Jacob then made a decision to make amends with his original enemy,

his older brother Esau.

After returning home, Jacob and his brother Esau,
each seeing one another for who they truly were—
brothers through and through—

joyfully put to bed
their past rivalry
and emotionally reconciled
in a touching, tearful embrace.

In the end, the two brothers
would find it in their hearts
to forgive one another
in spite of the rivalrous conflict.

THE GENESIS OF VIOLENCE

On this day,
love would triumph over hate.
These brothers,

initially
full of
impulsivity and deception,

in the end
would turn to
grace and mercy,

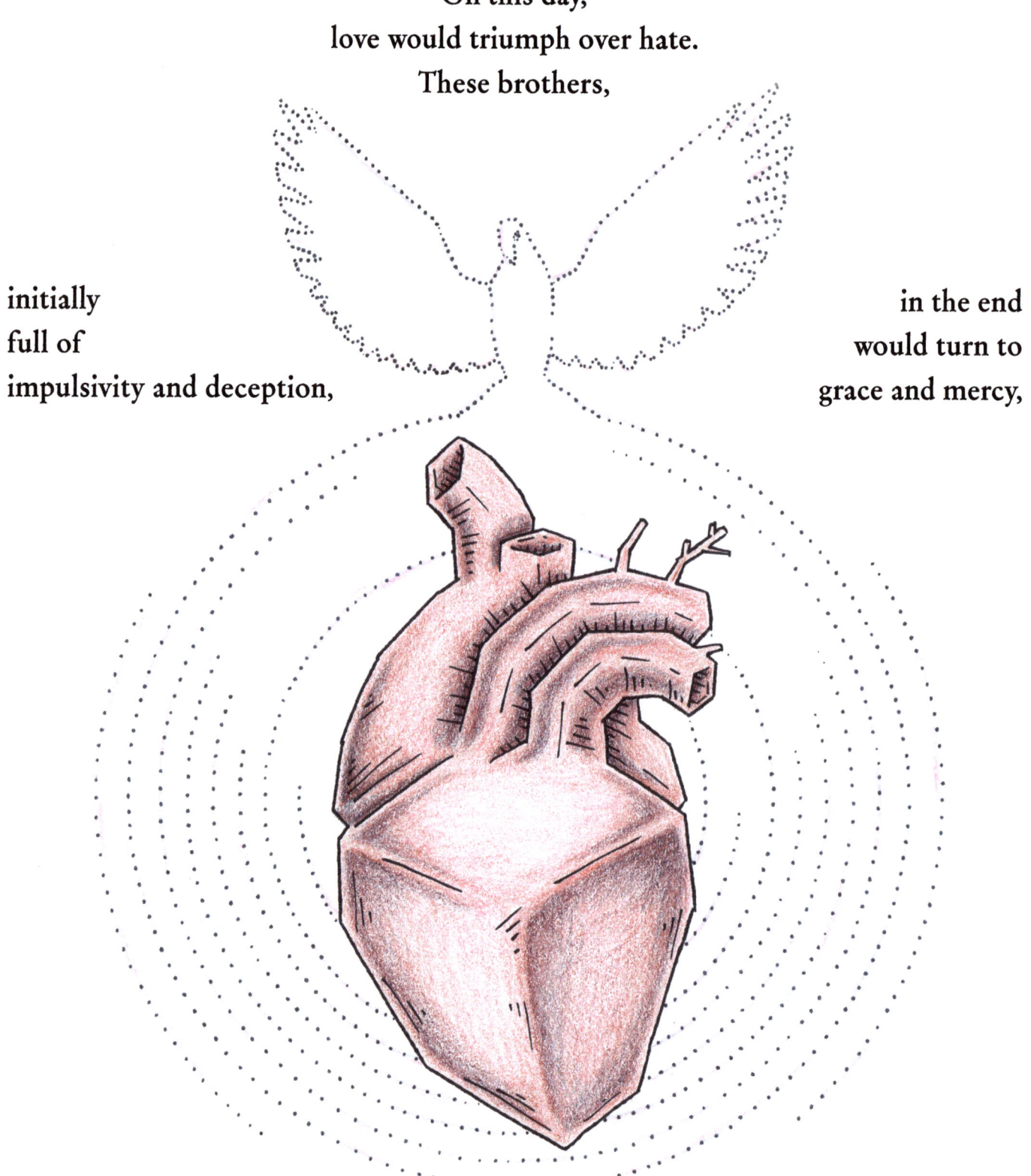

which again greatly pleased the Creator,
and She saw it as good.

CHAPTER V

Treachery and Reconciliation

Just one generation later, the family crisis would again be rekindled.
The most beloved of Jacob's sons was Joseph,
who, because of his father's extra affection, was hated by all of his brothers.
This made Joseph stand out as the cause of any of their problems.

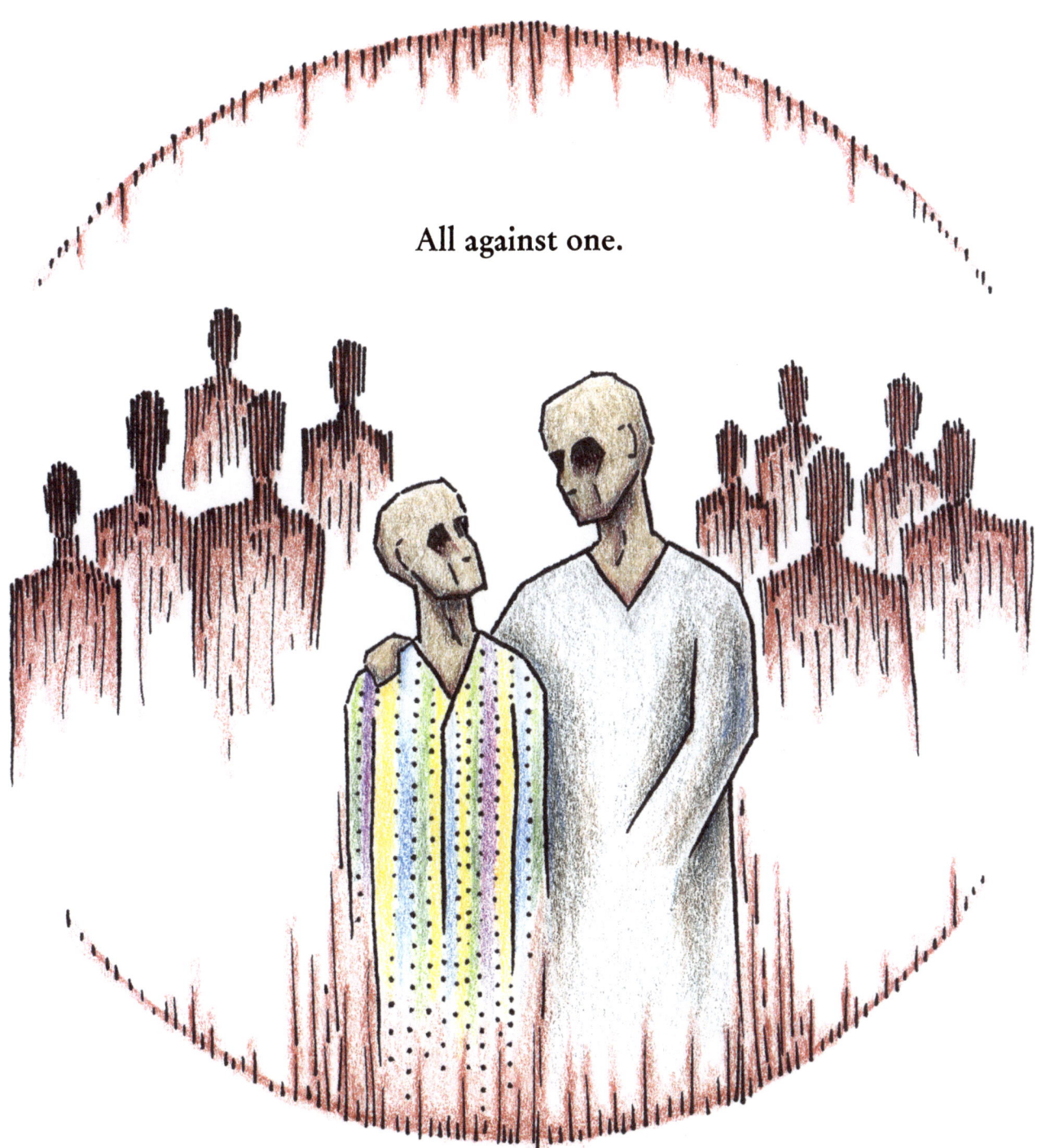

All against one.

The brothers' envy made it impossible for them to love Joseph.

THE GENESIS OF VIOLENCE

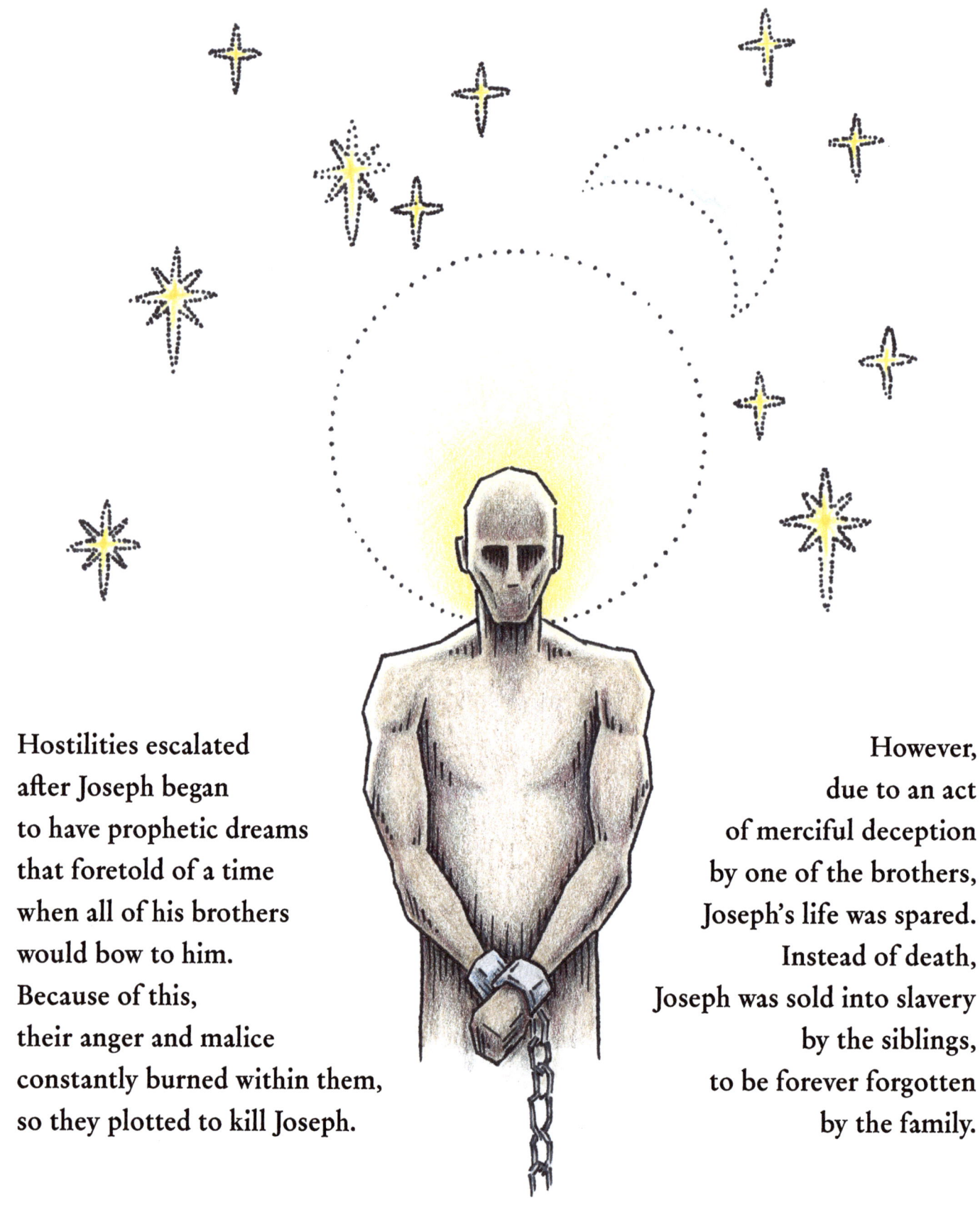

Hostilities escalated after Joseph began to have prophetic dreams that foretold of a time when all of his brothers would bow to him. Because of this, their anger and malice constantly burned within them, so they plotted to kill Joseph.

However, due to an act of merciful deception by one of the brothers, Joseph's life was spared. Instead of death, Joseph was sold into slavery by the siblings, to be forever forgotten by the family.

Or so they thought ...

After Joseph fell into the hands of the Egyptians,
he was quickly deceived and found himself in prison
under false pretenses.

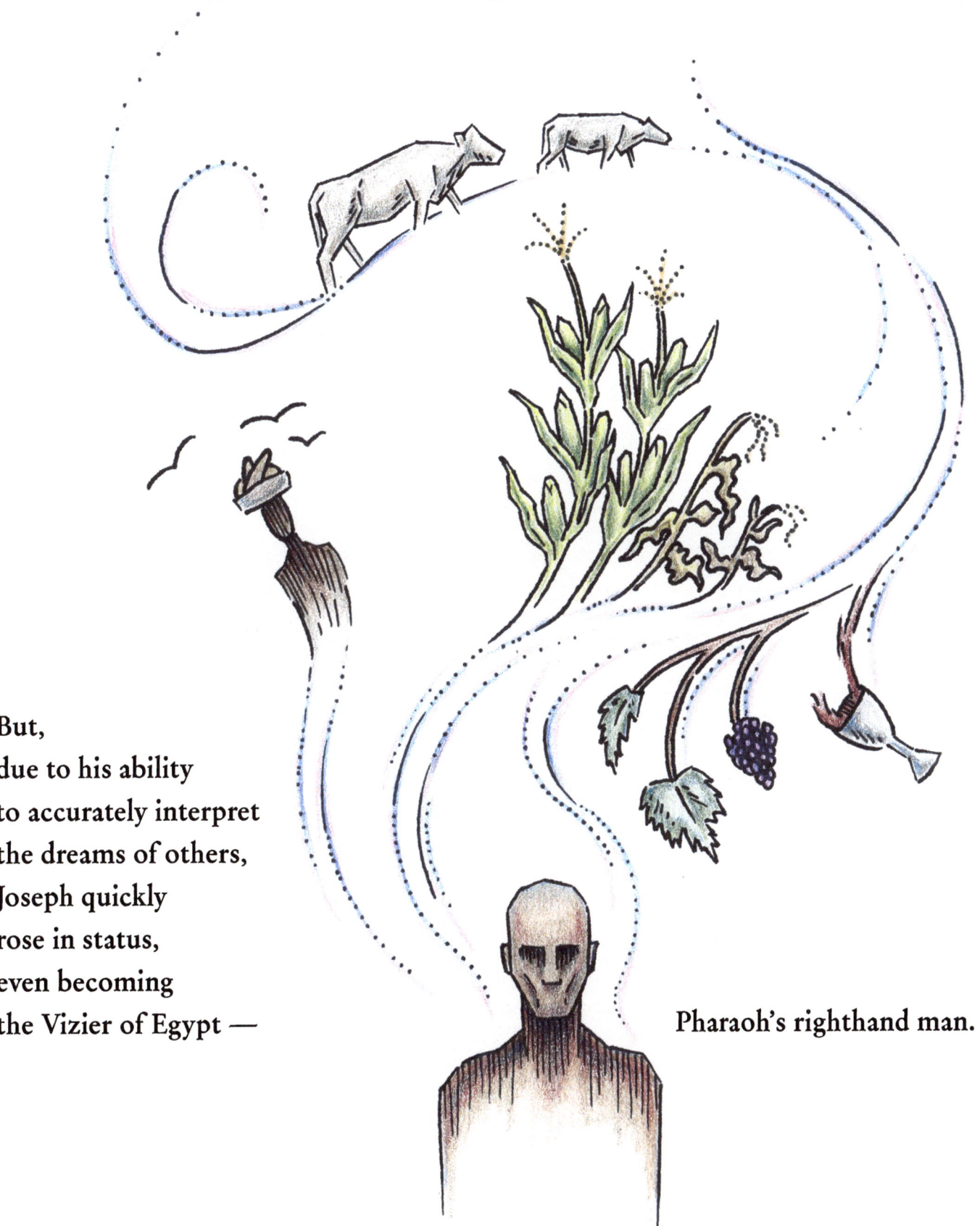

But,
due to his ability
to accurately interpret
the dreams of others,
Joseph quickly
rose in status,
even becoming
the Vizier of Egypt —

Pharaoh's righthand man.

THE GENESIS OF VIOLENCE

During this time, there was a great famine in the land.

It was so severe that people from afar had to travel to the prosperous Egypt
in order to   to feed
purchase grain   their family.

Joseph, as Vizier,
was entrusted by Pharaoh
to be in charge of the stores of crops.

One day, starving, some of Joseph's brothers came to purchase grain from the Egyptians.

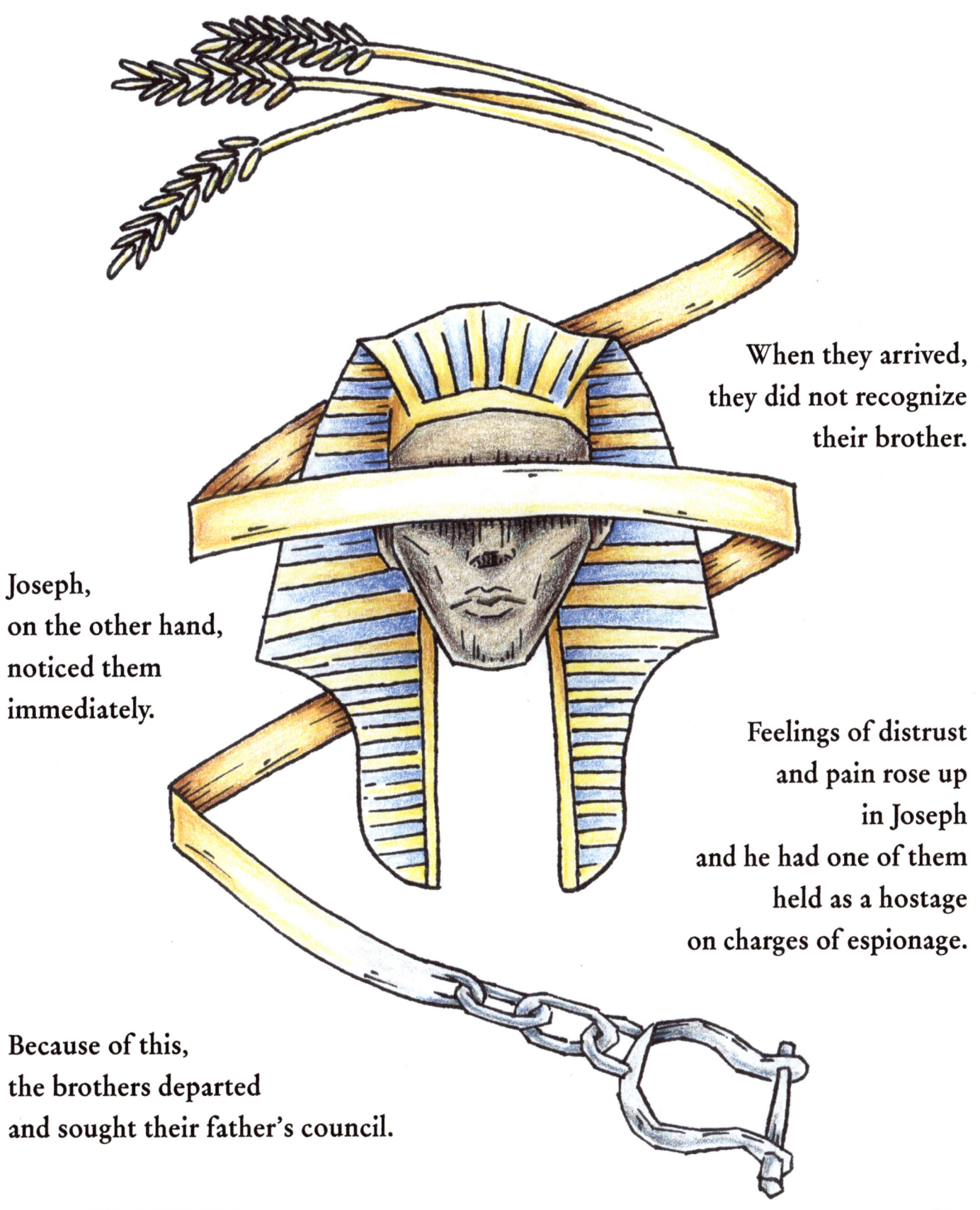

When they arrived, they did not recognize their brother.

Joseph, on the other hand, noticed them immediately.

Feelings of distrust and pain rose up in Joseph and he had one of them held as a hostage on charges of espionage.

Because of this, the brothers departed and sought their father's council.

THE GENESIS OF VIOLENCE

After the brothers convinced their father to allow Benjamin,
the youngest of them, to aid in the hostage situation,
they returned to Egypt.

Initially, they were met by Joseph with graciousness.
However, after the cordial introduction,
one that most assuredly gave the brothers confidence
that they had at last earned the Vizier's favor,
Joseph went on the offensive.

Unbeknownst to the brothers,
Joseph hid a silver cup in Benjamin's sack,
with the intentions of unfairly detaining him.

Then, after they left,
Joseph sent a steward in hot pursuit.
After the cup was found,
the brothers were immediately brought back to Joseph,
who was eagerly awaiting their return.

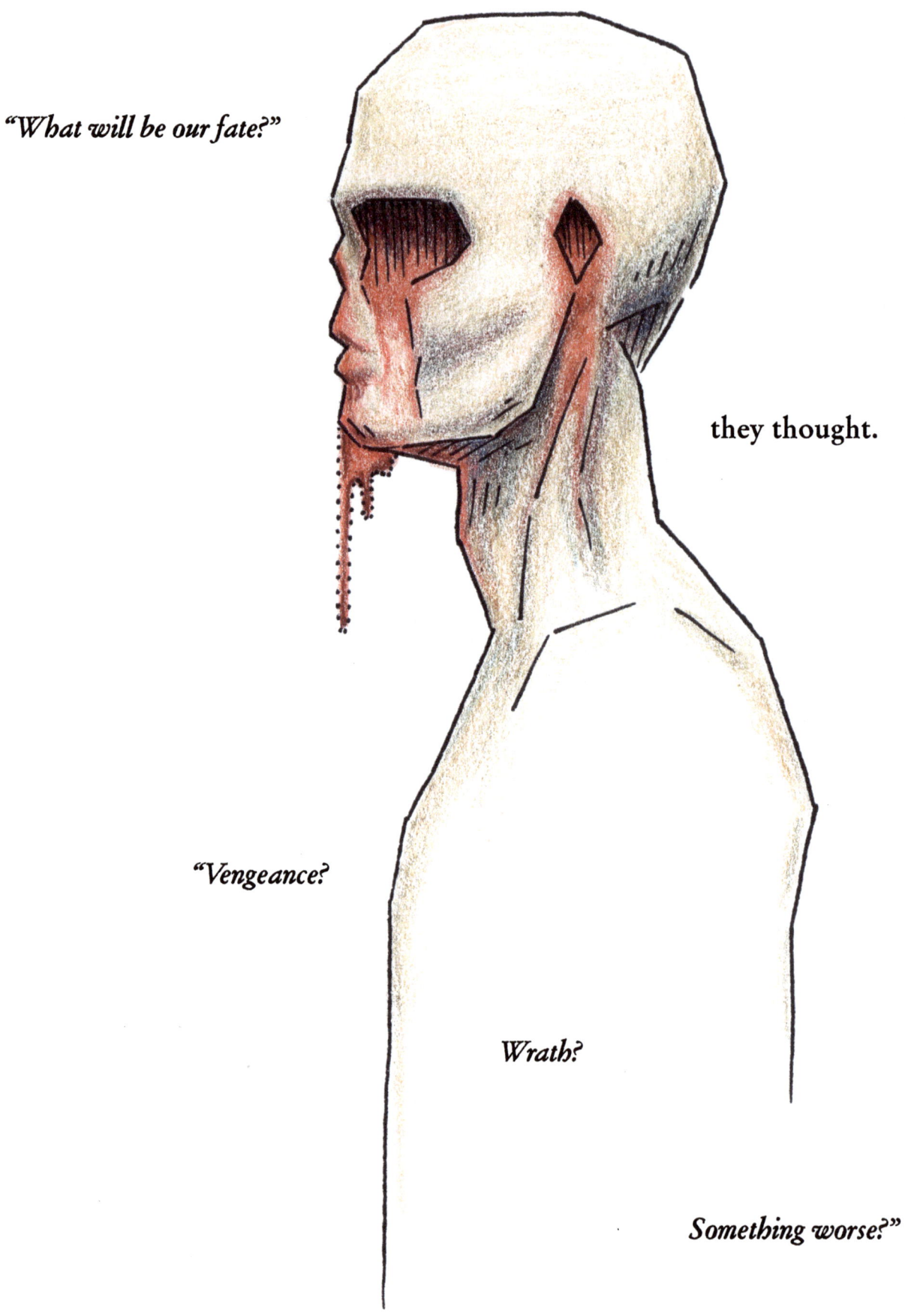

But that was not what Joseph had in mind.

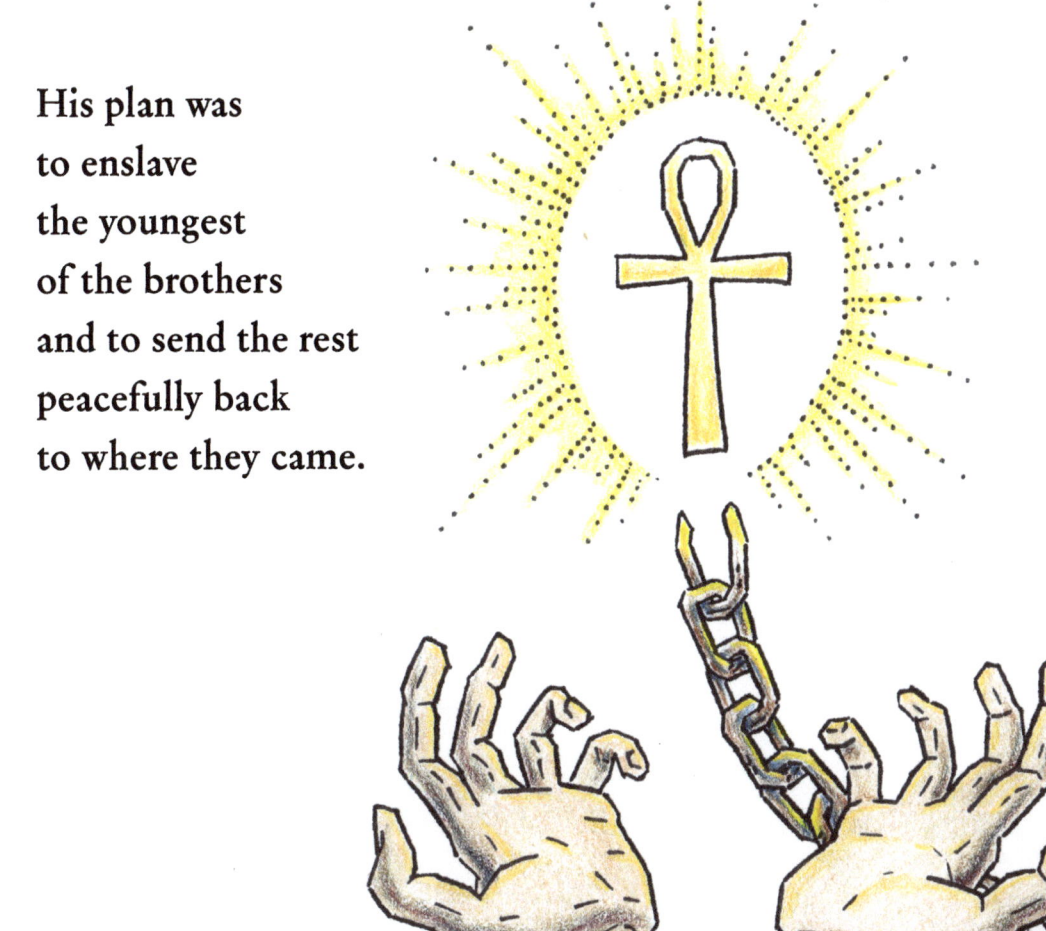

His plan was
to enslave
the youngest
of the brothers
and to send the rest
peacefully back
to where they came.

However, Judah,
one of the
older brothers,
begged and pleaded
for Joseph to release
Benjamin and to
keep him instead.

It was an act
of self-sacrifice,
a free giving of one's self
for the benefit of the other.

THE GENESIS OF VIOLENCE

Something extraordinary then took place.

Joseph broke down and wept, revealing his true identity to his treacherous brothers. No longer could he keep up his game of charades. Immediately, Joseph sent for his father so that he, along with the entire family, could settle in Egypt, embrace prosperity, and reunite as a family.

In the minds of the brothers, this type of grace and mercy was confounding.

Sometime after the family settled in the land, Jacob died.
But before he did, he gave his blessing

to Joseph 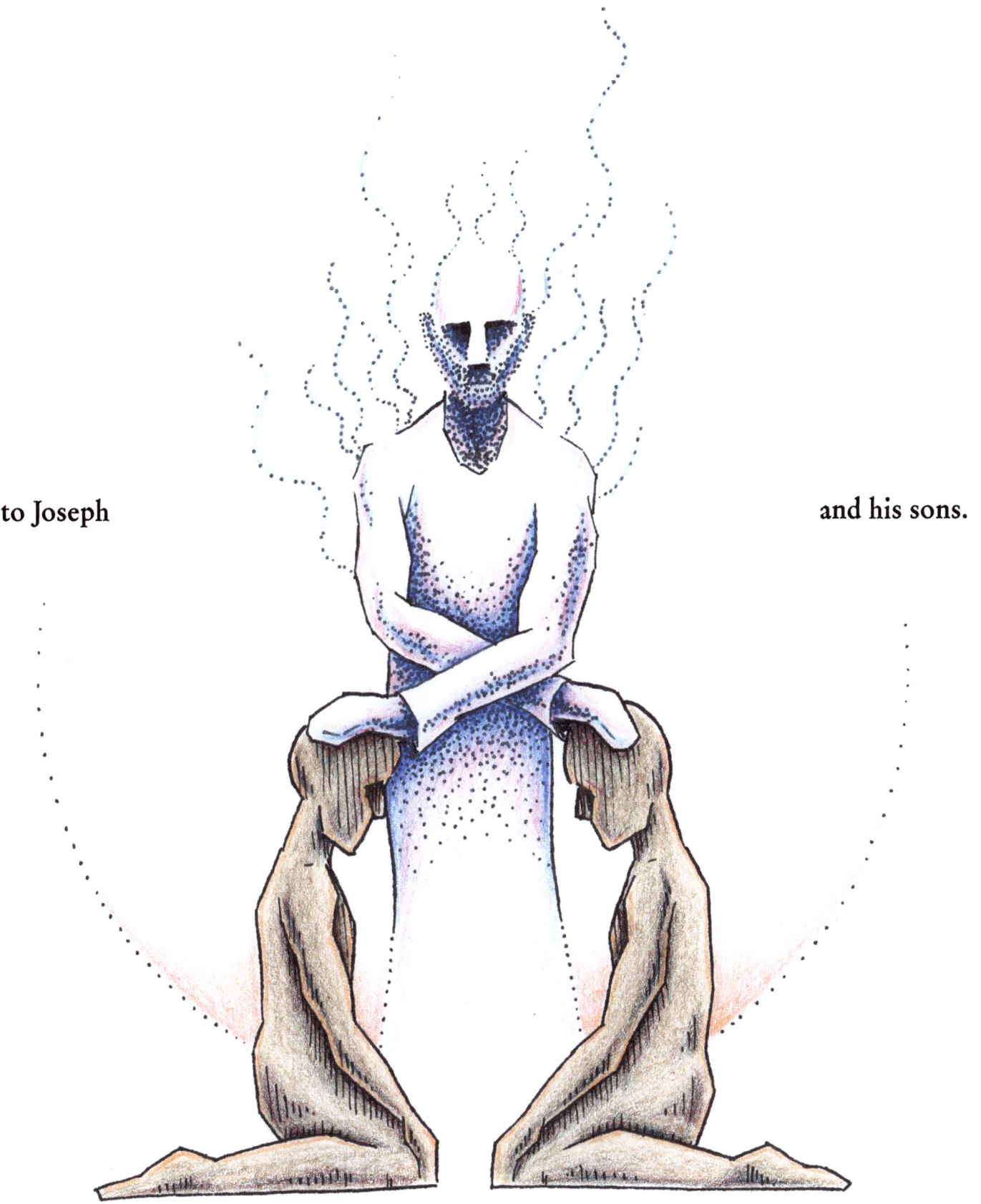 and his sons.

THE GENESIS OF VIOLENCE

This worried Joseph's brothers, however, as they all believed
it was now likely that Joseph would finally have his long-awaited revenge.
Humbly, they all approached the sibling they had wronged
and asked for forgiveness for their original treachery.
Joseph, who was weeping the entire time, graciously offered them the following:

*"Even though you intended to do harm to me, the Creator intended it for good,
in order to preserve a multitude of people, including you.
So have no fear; I myself will provide for you and your little ones."*

Because of this grace—
    this beautiful grace—
all of Joseph's brothers
then fell down
and offered themselves
as servants.

Without force or coercion, but rather, through the power of uncoercive love and mercy, the prophecy that Joseph would be served by all of his siblings came true.

The family drama, which began generations prior in the mountains of Moriah, would conclude with all of them being reconciled through the weakness of unadulterated grace.

And this pleased the Creator evermore, and She saw that it was very good.

THE GENESIS OF VIOLENCE

Matthew J. Distefano

Matthew J. Distefano is the author of *Heretic!* and 4 other books. He is a podcaster and columnist for Patheos, as well as a long-time social worker. He lives in Northern California with his wife and daughter.

Zak D. Parsons

Zak D. Parsons has always had a love of symbolic and abstract art. *The Genesis of Violence* is his first illustrated book project. He lives in the DMV area with his wife and their four children. You can find more of his work at zakdp.com

For more information about Matthew J. Distefano
please visit *www.AllSetFree.com*

For more information about Zak D. Parsons
please visit *www.ZakDP.com*

Many voices. One message.

Quoir is a boutique publisher
with a singular message: *Christ is all.*
Venture beyond your boundaries to discover Christ
in ways you never thought possible.

For more information, please visit
www.quoir.com

www.ingramcontent.com/pod-product-compliance
Lightning Source LLC
Chambersburg PA
CBHW040800240426
43673CB00015B/404